There are so many people to thank and to whom this book could be dedicated, but most important are my trans ancestors and community around the world, without whom my existence could never be real. I dedicate this book to all those who have gone before me with power and pride and paved the way.

Also to the people who supported and allowed these performances to come to life. Through producing, offering space, creative input, love and inspiration. As an artist, I only want to work in a context of collaboration, and this work would have been literally impossible without the amazing people who sat with me in rehearsal rooms, offered support and provocation and lent their extraordinary talents. Extra special thanks to Abby Butcher, Myriddin Pharo, Ivor MacAskill, Keir Cooper and Rachel Mars.

And finally, I dedicate this to Joey, who was born at the very beginning of this project. I am so proud to be your Daddy.

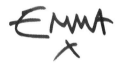

First published in 2019 by Oberon Books Ltd
521 Caledonian Road, London N7 9RH
Tel: +44 (0) 20 7607 3637 / Fax: +44 (0) 20 7607 3629
e-mail: info@oberonbooks.com
www.oberonbooks.com

Designed by Konstantinos Vasdekis

Cover artwork by Will Brady

Photography © Steve Tanner (back cover, introduction); Rosie Powell (introduction, *Language*, *Rituals for Change*, *Hearty*); Adam Young (*Language*); Julia Bauer (*e g g / b o x*); David Monteith-Hodge (*Rituals for Change*); Maurizio Martorana (*Hearty*); Joshua Pharo (*Hearty*).

Illustrations © Emma Frankland (*Doodle*); Myriddin Pharo (*Hearty*).

Printed and bound by Replika Press PVT LTD, India.

I lay claim to the irreducible plurality of my living body, not to my body as 'bare life', but to the very materiality of my body as a political site for agency and resistance.

— **Paul B. Preciado,** *Testo Junkie*

Trans femmes are the
Past, present and future
We are all the
Possibilities ur world
Could be
We are deserving of
Your love, protection,
Affection

— **Travis Alabanza,**
***Before I Step Outside (You Love Me)***

Ela tem cara de mulher.
Ela tem corpo de mulher
Ela tem jeito
Tem bunda
Tem peito
E o pau de mulher!

— **Linn da Quebrada, 'Mulher'**

# FOREWORD / BEFORE WE WERE NOT YET ROBOTS

*In the world before, a woman thrashes about the stage singing about complex trans women. 'If you are in possession of a penis you are not allowed to be in possession of... Gracefulness!'*

*In the world before, a grown woman – grown in the sense of having reached adulthood, though she is only a baby in the trans sense – reads and recites inside a cardboard box.*

*In the world after, a woman draws conversations with strangers in public, putting a frame around the everyday negotiations of bodies and gender and politics that pass by any given space in this after-world.*

*In the world after, a woman swings an axe up above her pinned-down hand, pulling back from chopping it off at precisely the last moment.*

*In the world after, much after, a woman with sharp wings drinks horse piss as a means of survival.*

This cycle of performance works by British trans artist Emma Frankland hinges chronologically around the seismic shift in cultural conversation on the rights and lives of trans people crystallised in the May 2014 *TIME* Magazine cover that announced – whether we were ready for it or not, whether it was of our own creation or merely a convenient story for a media looking for the next new controversy in a post-gay marriage America – a 'Transgender Tipping Point'. Laverne Cox, stunning in a blue bandage dress, ushered in what has been called derisively on this side of the pond a 'Genderquake' that has upended not only the everyday lives of trans people but also the culture at large.

'We've been here before,' Frankland reminds us in *Hearty*, repeated as a mantra to ward off the forgetfulness of the apocalypse. And she's right: whether during the 1950s when Christine Jorgensen stepped a well-turned heel out onto the tarmac at what is now JFK Airport in New York to the delight of a media frenzy, or in the 70s when trans sex workers of colour like Sylvia Rivera and Marsha P. Johnson helped usher in a gender revolution wrapped inside the sexual revolution, we have been here before. Just as then, we have in the past seven years gained unprecedented new rights and acceptance across Western societies, and then watched a vicious backlash – led in grinning partnership by extreme right-wing Evangelicals, British tabloids, and a minority of anti-trans feminists – dismantle those same rights and attack the very premise of our existence.

Frankland's work, collected here for the first time, skilfully articulates what it means to be a – white, British – trans person in these troubled times. Here we find both fear and laughter, her protagonists balancing on the precipice like The Fool from the tarot. She suggests possibility and danger.

But again, she reminds us: 'We've been here before.' Resisting the drive to what might be called 'trans exceptionalism' ('the first trans to give birth,' 'the first trans to win an Oscar,' 'the first trans to walk on the Moon,' etcetera), Frankland crucially locates her work in dialogue with that of other artists – such as Imogen Binnie, whose novel *Nevada* is quoted at the start of *Language*, or Paul B. Preciado, whose magnum opus *Testo Junkie* can be seen inside the *e g g / b o x*. Her work draws on a vital history of trans performance – from Mirha-Soleil Ross to Nina Arsenault, Aiyyana Maracle to Cassils, Vaginal Davis to Tobaron Waxman – helping further an emerging canon that in this after-world may no longer be ignored.

As we weather a backlash that threatens to erase our existence, we look towards our artists, both for balm and for oracular guidance, and it is within these ritual performance works of Emma Frankland that we are able to find them.

**— Morgan M Page, March 2019**

# INTRODUCTION

# 'WE ARE ALL **BIOLOGICAL,** NONE OF US **IS YET A ROBOT'**

This book collects the texts of five live perfor-mance and theatre pieces, created under the project title *None of Us is Yet a Robot* between 2012 and 2019 – *Language*, *Doodle*, *e g g / b o x*, *Rituals for Change* and *Hearty*. Each work is a solo piece, performed originally by me and made in response to my gender transition and the political events and emotions surrounding me at that time.

Naming the project became a necessity after a listings magazine published a description of my first show as a 'journey from a man to a woman' alongside my name. Not only was this reductive (and what the show was directly challenging), but it was before I had even come out to my family. The name *None of Us is Yet a Robot* felt like a safety blanket, something to hide behind while I changed. It was an early lesson in the way that the media seek to sensationalise trans people and centre our stories on a transitional moment only, and it is strange to remember a time when my shame was stronger than my sense of pride.

The name itself is a comment on a slur that is often thrown at trans women – that cis women are 'biological' and we are not. An endocrinologist I interviewed for the project once told me that 'being trans is just an innate part of human diversity,' which seems a fairly obvious truth. Trans people are biological. We exist; we have always existed; we always will. What *does* change over time is mainstream acceptance (or lack thereof) and the amount of persecution and violence we face as a result.

It's hard to comprehend how much has changed in a few short years, both in my personal life and in the broader public attitude to trans people – so much that I find the timeline hard to hold onto. I was introduced to the concept of 'queer time' a few years ago during the rehearsal process for Jo Clifford's *Every One* – and to be a transsexual is definitely to inhabit a queer timeline. Like many others who have bodies that take non-normative routes or have medical interventions, our timeline is altered. And like a transsexual Sam Beckett from *Quantum Leap*, we effectively time travel within our own lifetime: puberty, adolescence, menopause, all coming out of order, smashing together and flying apart.

When I focus on my own timeline, it all seems unreal – how can a moment only be three years ago, when it feels like a lifetime? How can another moment have happened twenty years ago, when last year the same thing occured? How could there have been a time when I could describe my gender on stage but feel unable to tell my parents?

# TO BE TRANS
## IS TO BE
# A TIME TRAVELLER.

I feel like I have had the longest transition of anyone that ever lived, but I know that's not the case: I recently met an eighty-nine-year-old trans woman who began her transition aged eighty-six. Being trans is not just a trend reserved for the young. It's been a long journey (far longer than the focus of this book) between first articulating how I felt to finally feeling at peace in my body – not to mention the years when I knew, but could not articulate it. I was making concessions for other people. I was afraid of the repercussions. If I regret anything, it is that I didn't trust myself sooner.

I first called this project *Small Things* because at one stage my transition felt like it was a series of small things that added up step by step. This was how I articulated it when the project began, when it was still impossible to believe I'd end up here. It was impossible to imagine that trans people would ever come out of the shadows, let alone be demanding mainstream acceptance and human rights. I felt sure that, at the very least, transition would mean an end to my performance career. I could not know that I would perform my work across the UK and in different parts of the world, meeting many incredible trans (including non-binary) people along the way. It was hard to believe

I would ever feel comfortable and valid in calling myself a woman.

Today, it is hard to remember that being trans ever felt unnatural and shameful and hard. That it was ever in question that I am a woman. Of course I can remember those years; but like recalling the pain of a broken arm, it is a hard feeling to embody again. Today, I feel so complete and obvious and comfortable. Today I feel so ordinary...

So I am trying to think about beginnings and I am trying to be honest and honour the process of making these five performances. A process that was messy and difficult and sometimes a little embarrassing. A process in which, among other things, I articulated for the first time my understanding of the role of an artist. I was inspired by a pool lifeguard manual that I had studied as a teenager when I worked as a lifeguard at my local leisure centre in Cornwall. The book articulates the 'duty of care' of a lifeguard: you must rescue someone you see drowning even if you aren't getting paid to do so. I love the idea of a 'duty of care', of a social responsibility to one's community and the world around us. So I asked myself – what do I believe is the duty of care of an artist?

Then, as now, I believe it is to be honest and bold and to respond to the world as we truthfully experience it. This does not mean we cannot be perverse or silly or playful (I reserve the right to be all these things) but it means that we must not ignore or sugarcoat the realities of our own existence. Not pander to mainstream representation that harms others in our community in order to make ourselves secure. This duty of care gave the work a sense of purpose; clarity about why I should be articulating my journey as a trans woman.

I believe that to be a trans person is to be a person with an essential role in a balanced and harmonious society – a notion that has been reinforced on each occasion I have spent time with trans women from other cultures. Much of our ancient understanding has been occluded by our comparatively recent colonial history, but in contemporary Western culture we are at a point of great rediscovery and potential healing – what *TIME* Magazine named in 2014 as the 'Transgender Tipping Point' and what Paul Preciado calls a gender revolution:

**'The gender binary regime is undergoing a major crisis...some of our lives are the material proof of this gender revolution. So at the same time that we are really in a moment of epistemic crisis, we are also living a moment of counter-revolution.'**

It is clear that we are also in a period of global political turmoil. It is 2019 and in the UK we experience slander and attack from mainstream media and anti-trans pressure groups almost daily. There is great uncertainty for trans and LGBQ people around the world.

And yet, personally... Things are so, so much better than I could ever have hoped for in my whole life.

**Trans women are radical. To be a trans woman is a political act.**

**To be a proud trans woman is to blow the system apart.**

To walk down the street as a trans woman is a political act, but I do not believe in the benefit of visibility at all costs. We exist against all odds and despite the challenges. Poet and editor Cat Fitzpatrick once explained to me that while trans women have historically been targets of violence, the motivations behind the attacks are now changing. Now that we have more visibility, trans people are being painted as a credible threat – and as well as collecting allies we have also gained forceful opponents. So there is necessity for caution, which can be difficult in the pervasive atmosphere of a media who bombard trans people with offers to 'debate' our existence against people who do not believe our truth. I think there is power in rejecting a platform, in refusing to legitimise a toxic point of view disguised as debate. What is desperately needed are forums for trans people to speak our own truths and share our history and our stories with each other. I am reluctant to call myself an activist (though others may insist on doing so), preferring to follow Kate Bornstein's description of herself as 'an artist in service of activism' – as such, I attempt to use whatever platform being a performer provides me with to do this.

California becomes the first US state to ban 'trans panic' as a legal defense. A private doctor gives me the diagnosis of 'transsexual'.

As I say in *Rituals for Change*: 'The radical act is to exist, the radical act is to be seen, to choose to allow others to see these radical bodies – to allow ourselves to heal is the radical act.'

So there was a beginning to this project, although I am not sure when it became a project rather than a single show. Or anything beyond a process of personal articulation. But I know that at some point the total sum of these five productions became something more coherent than the individual parts. I know how reductive it is to look at this timeline as a linear series of events, because some moments came almost overnight while others had been brewing forever. It will be tempting to read this book and consider, for example, that I only 'transitioned' in 2014 (when I changed my name and started taking magic hormone pills) – but to do this would be to undermine the reality that I have always been a trans woman. A key concept in *Rituals for Change* is that it is inherently flawed to choose one moment over another. Things that occurred in 2014, while significant, were but the tip of an extremely long iceberg... Or probably not even the tip. There can be no such thing as a tip, or a tipping point. We are not mountaineers, we are tightrope walkers. We step delicately backwards and forwards along our timelines...

**To be trans is to be a time traveller.**

I perform *Doodle* and *e g g / b o x* at Forest Fringe and begin taking oestrogen in the form of small blue pills. Facebook expand their

pronouns, but choose to remain 'Daddy' to Jowan. **2015** I perform an updated version

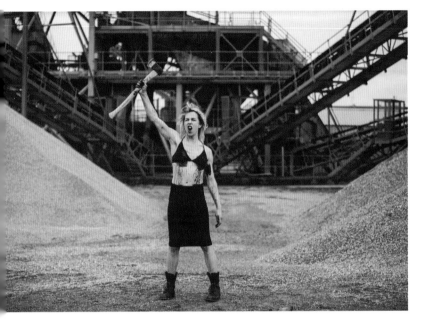

of *Language* at CPT which is bolder, messier and louder. The project becomes *None of Us is Yet a Robot*. Stonewall officially begin

# SOME MOMENTS THAT HAVE **STOOD OUT** IN **MY MEMORY** WHEN PUTTING **TOGETHER THIS BOOK...**

I am telling the second person ever that I am transgender. I start speaking and my words freeze – I literally cannot speak. We sit in silence for about five minutes, my mouth opening and closing. She is the first person I will tell who gives me a positive response, asks me how I am. Tells me I am ok.

I am dressed up to go out to a club night marketed towards men who crossdress. I come home with a friend and we sit and talk about how, rather than be forced to go to clubs like that, we wish we could just live like this day to day. The thought feels like the most exotic and impossible thing and I feel sick when I think about it. 'My life is so good,' I think. 'My life is so perfect. Just hold on and don't let this be a thing.'

Crying in rehearsal because for the first time I could admit how significant clothes were to me, and because the desire of it all was too much to bear. Aged thirty-three, I wore a skirt I bought when I was fourteen for the first time.

Wearing a beautiful set of metal wings fashioned from sharp knives. Learning how to wear them so they do not cut my back to ribbons. It feels like a rite of passage.

> Staying up all night painting a billboard that reads: 'We are a Hearty Sisterhood.'

> Staying up all night the following night because of a terrible argument.

Walking into long, wet grass in a Highland dawn to conduct a ritual for my female ancestors, asking permission and acceptance. The playlist I created for this was 'All Apologies' by Nirvana (covered by Sinead O'Connor), 'Modern Girl' by Sleater-Kinney, and 'Feeling Good' by Nina Simone. This is an excellent playlist for a ritual.

> Crouching behind a bin on Brighton beach to shelter from the wind whilst having a phone conversation with Myriddin Pharo about ritual and ancestors that formed the entire basis for *Rituals for Change*.

Telling Ira Brand that *Rituals for Change* would be a 'clean show with no mess.'

Breaking that promise.

> Walking into long, wet grass in South Sulawesi alongside a group of Bissu shamans to conduct a ritual in a sacred cave asking for safety for our community, and honouring the trans people (calabai and calalai – transfeminine and trans-masculine) who hid from persecution in that cave only fifty years previously.

Performing in Leeds to a self-identified trans-only audience and feeling liberated. I dropped the blanket covering my breasts as I realised that I did not need to hide or explain my body to anyone in that room. Making clay pots together and talking with the audience afterwards.

Literally every conversation with a trans person after one of my performances.

Sitting with a cis woman who has devoted her life to studying the menopause. Having a beautiful and exciting conversation about what menopause might look like for a trans woman that resulted in the commission of an official academic study.

The feeling of putting on thick red lipstick and feeling powerful, and then seeing someone else's face and feeling the power turn to shame...which is powerful in a different way.

A heckler at a conference in Brazil saying something with such clarity that I am trying to honour it still.

Holding a ritual space for Trans Day of Remembrance in São Paulo, where we wrote in chalk and then washed away the names of people killed for being (or being thought to be) transgender in the previous twelve months. It was supposed to be one person washing away the names, but others spontaneously joined in, supporting each other – some using their clothes as cloths to carefully clean the ground.

All of the small moments. The day I turned my belt in the opposite direction (I had been told that women wear them buckled to the right); wearing eyeliner outside for the first time and people thinking I had become a rock star; shaving my legs for the first time. Each of these 'small moments' felt HUGE.

Making clay sculptures with a group of trans women in Jakarta, Indonesia, and them asking me: 'Where in the world are we safe and valued?' Performing *Rituals for Change* there later that week and feeling the importance of the line 'REVOLUTION NOW.'

Witnessing a cis man square up to my travesti friend on the streets of São Paulo while the world moved on around us.

Learning to be afraid when walking through the streets at night and then trying to learn again how not to be.

Jokingly forming a trans caucus in Canada with two Two-Spirit artists and feeling like we were the secret global trans conspiracy come true.

A calabai Bissu shaman in South Sulawesi inviting me to join a ritual. Her tears of joy as she saw my ancestors and felt secure in my motive for coming to her. She said she never knew there were calabai outside of Sulawesi.

Finding strength in my trans sisters.

2017 I begin training with Brighton Rockers Roller Derby and working on *Hearty* in the same week. Performance artist Travis

Alabanza becomes a media target after being refused entry to female changing rooms in Topshop. We receive funding from the Wellcome

# HOW TO USE THIS BOOK

I WANT THIS BOOK TO BE **A TIME CAPSULE** AS WELL AS **A COLLECTION OF PLAY TEXTS** / TO SERVE AS AN EXAMPLE FOR A **TRANS PERSON** LOOKING TO **FIND SOMEONE LIKE THEMSELVES** / TO EXIST AS PROOF THAT **THIS JOURNEY IS POSSIBLE** / TO BE **A SNAPSHOT OF CONTEMPORARY THEATRE PRACTICE** IN THE EARLY TWENTY-FIRST CENTURY / AND **TO BE VISIBLE, TO EXIST**

I identify as a trans woman, but I do not presume to represent the complexities of other trans identities. I am also a white, able-bodied woman from the UK, and want to avoid any appearance of presenting my experience as some sort of universal standard. As Morgan M Page wrote on her Buzzfeed blog:

**'As many black feminists – like [Dr] Kimberlé Crenshaw, who coined the term 'intersectionality' – have been pointing out for decades, race and class divisions create a such variety of life experiences that we can only come to view the idea of a singular experience of girlhood and womanhood as a myth. No one is actually saying trans women and cis women's experiences are exactly the same – and that's because no two women's experiences are exactly the same. There is not one womanhood, but many.'**

Here are five performance texts presented as they were performed on five specific occasions. Each performance had a broader life, was also seen in other contexts and with different words. They are living scripts, and because of how rapidly language and politics around trans lives have shifted in the last seven years, it often felt necessary to update them. But each version included in this book feels definitive. I will place each text in its time and context – both in my head and in the world.

I have conducted a series of interviews with artists and friends who were integral to the making of each piece and whose opinions and thoughts I value greatly. Elements of these conversations will be quoted for context and the whole conversations can be heard online as a podcast series.

I perform as part of an all-trans cast in *Summer in London at Theatre Royal Stratford East*. **2018** *Rituals* is made into a film.

I invite the cis reader to read, consider and take action in support of trans rights.

I invite the trans reader to feel loved and seen. To feel free to criticise and to feel encouraged to write your own words and to read further, to uncover our history and all that has gone before.

I invite the performer and artist to use these words as you see fit; to quote, borrow, or repeat.

And I invite the programmer to ask me to perform these works for as long as they feel relevant. To pay me and to provide an audience.

I will be making more work as an artist. It is 2019 and my practice feels young – I am visiting other countries and collaborating with other trans people. My world is expanding and I want to make performances for larger stages and to share those spaces with multiple bodies – to see trans artists collaborating and performing together, not just in solo shows.

**But this volume represents the *None of Us is Yet a Robot* project, as it ran from 2012 to 2019.**

exclusionary lesbians, and the hashtag #LwiththeT is coined. I am discharged from my

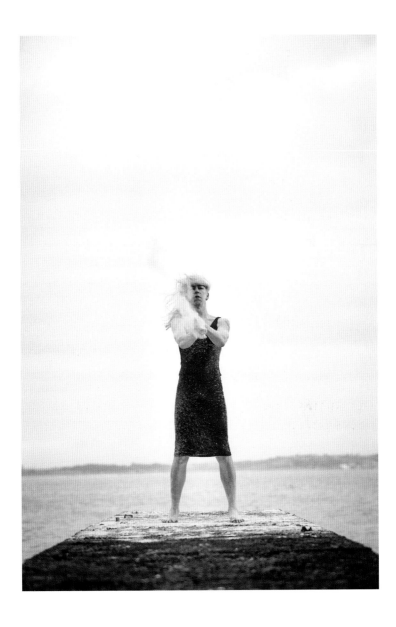

# Language

In conversation with Rachel Mars, November 2018
Performance text: Camden People's Theatre, March 2015

'I've never managed to perform *Language* dispassionately, in a way that I have been able to do with other pieces. With *Language* it was always... It was always a bit hot. Just in terms of what it was to stand on a stage and be. In a way that it wouldn't be now, 'cause I'm just Emma, everyone knows me as Emma, I'm trans, whatever – but back then... They didn't.'

*'What is your show about?'*
*'Myself, I guess.'*
*'Well, I hope that you are interesting.'*

This conversation took place on the very first morning of the first Research & Development period for this project, which took place at Ovalhouse Theatre in South London in July 2012. I was asked what the show would be about by the person at the box office. Their response filled me with dread and self-doubt... *Was* I interesting? Was transition an *interesting* subject? What sort of space was I taking up by entertaining these notions, and whose voice might I be silencing by using valuable resources?

I was joined in the room by Rachel Mars, who describes herself as '"she" with a "they" inflection.' Rachel's work had been seminal to me the previous year at the Edinburgh Fringe festival, where I saw their show *Tomboy Blues (or the Theory of Disappointment)*, co-devised with Rachel's long-time performance partner Nat Tarrab. At the time I was desperate to see myself reflected and to hear trans stories, and so I had been scanning the festival brochure for any shows referencing gender, whilst at the same time feeling terrified about what I might give away about myself by doing so. I was incredibly moved by the performance – although it wasn't framed as a trans story, it explored female masculinity, tomboy desire...and pants.

A promotional wristband given to the audience after the show became a sort of talisman for me, and I started wearing it regularly – then one day it flipped inside out and revealed a secret message, embossed on the inside: 'You can wear whatever pants you want.' At that time (the summer of 2011) this message provided a huge amount of relief from the feelings of guilt and dread I was carrying around. It was a tremendous gift.

As a theatre-maker, it seemed sensible to explore the feelings I was experiencing. Securing a little support from Ovalhouse, I invited Rachel to help facilitate the process. These early explorations would ultimately become *Language* – but not for several years.

> **RACHEL** You were wearing a bowler hat and cowboy boots, and you were doing that show with your dad. Even those decisions I think were quite big for you, like the bowler hat and the cowboy boots. I remember we then reflected that that was actually a big step that you'd made.

> **EMMA** It's hard to think about how much lack of permission I felt to do things. Some of which was related with my personal situation, and looking after other people's sensibilities, and part of it is just how fucking hard it is to come out. The journey of coming out as a trans woman, of working out my identity as a queer trans woman – yeah, things that feel now really obvious... At the time I was just so worried about things that would give it away.

I filled the room with things in that first week. Toy Transformers robots from my childhood, my collection of *Blue Peter* annuals, an old lifeguard training manual. Clothes.

In that first development week, I remember writing lists; attempting to explain gender in the style of a *Blue Peter* presenter ('here's one I made earlier'); painting my nails. I remember crying for the first time in many years, when we finally stood in front of a mirror and Rachel asked questions about the significance of clothing. Standing in that room with Rachel was the first time in my life I'd felt seen as myself, and not judged or ashamed.

**EMMA** I remember the day we played with clothes. We'd been putting it off and putting it off...

**RACHEL** I remember that being quite a big thing, and the pain of that. You seeing yourself in the mirror, and the massive pain of that.

**EMMA** I remember that and I remember crying. Back then I didn't cry that much, now with hormones it's easier to cry, and I cry more often. There's more to cry about. But then, actually, crying was a surprising thing. And I remember on that afternoon just a lot of – a lot of – icky stuff coming out. And we didn't really put that into the show, 'cause it wasn't –

**RACHEL** No, that wasn't really necessary –

**EMMA** No, that was more for me. And that was huge, because up to that point all of the desire – which is just the desire to be true and to be actualised and seen and recognised – the only way that it had manifested had been under the terminology of 'crossdressing' and coming with a 'shame' connotation, or with a fetishised connotation. All these things that made me very uncomfortable. And also in a very cis, masculine, heteronormative world – the world of male crossdressing. And so it was probably the first time I was able to acknowledge those desires in front of another human being, and the response be like, 'Okay.'

Rachel set writing exercises and I attempted to articulate how I felt – how a lifetime of feeling like this had felt. I had been articulating my feelings about gender for some years, privately and with close friends. I had been reading a *lot* of books about gender theory (including books by Kate Bornstein, Julia Serano and Helen Boyd) and spent most of my free time reading articles and posts online. I had experienced several rounds of gender euphoria, but I was also in the grip of constant gender dysphoria. I hadn't been to my GP. I wasn't out. I hadn't changed my name. I was yet to change pronouns.

**RACHEL** Our work together wasn't easy – not because the making of the work wasn't easy, that was fruitful because there was so much to say and so much to think about and so many places to start – but the vital interpersonal stuff around it felt so hard. And heavy.

It is important to remember the nature of public discourse around trans lives at this time. In 2012 there was virtually no public discussion in the mainstream UK media around trans issues. The books I read were found on the internet and ordered mostly from North America. I would scour the gender studies shelf (never shelves) of bookshops, but rarely find a single book about trans experience except in specialist queer havens like Gay's the Word in London.

It seems convenient that the Western trans narrative exploded at the same time as my personal coming out, but I believe that's just a logical response to the internet coming of age, becoming accessible, and knowledge filtering through. Allowing us to understand ourselves from the shared experiences of others and not just through the lens of medical journals or Channel 4 documentaries that are mostly produced by cisgender white men. But certainly my coming out seemed to happen fractionally ahead of the avalanche of media and cultural interest in trans lives, which meant I did all of my own research in the dark – with a searchlight flicking on me at the time I felt most vulnerable. After more than a decade of searching to find myself reflected in obscure articles, internet chat rooms and photo sharing sites, it seemed like everyone suddenly had an opinion on what being trans meant.

**EMMA** I recall a moment – it was when we were working together – it was a Trans Day of Remembrance, six years ago, and I really hated the event. But I remember sitting there and having the realisation that – this isn't about other people. This is me. Just recognising myself as a trans woman, that was a huge thing.

And I guess what part of *None of Us is Yet a Robot* has done is try to be, I don't know – people came and saw the film last week and said, 'We saw this a few years ago and it was the first time we'd seen...' I get that, and I think we forget that you're not the last one to figure it out, and that there are still going to be people who are going to figure it out.

**RACHEL** You're not the last and you're not the first, and those two things are really important.

When I think back to 2012, I'm also struck by how young our language was. If you don't have a word to explain who or what you are, can you exist? One of the main reasons I didn't transition sooner was because, in 1990s Cornwall, my representation of trans women didn't stretch much beyond *The Crying Game* (where the response to discovering Dil is trans is for the protagonist to be violent and throw up). It felt important to see the words we were using as real – there were a lot of terms flying around and it was sometimes a fight to get words recognised. Later still in 2015, when I wrote an article for Lyn Gardner's *Guardian* blog, the editors requested that we remove the word 'cisgender' because it wasn't widely recognised. Ultimately, we included it with an explanation, and later that year it was added to the Oxford English Dictionary. Language was literally evolving in front of our eyes and transforming the conversation, the word 'cis' providing a way of explaining gender differences that did not fall into the trap of 'transgender' vs 'normal'.

We felt that what was needed was a sort of trans primer – there were plenty of trans 101 guides, but I wanted one that didn't just fixate on a binary, heteronormative story that focused on a moment of (supposedly inevitable) surgery. I wanted a primer that spoke of complexity, of the experience of trans women outside of a white, Eurocentric lens, and beyond the trapped-in-the-wrong-body trope that seemed to be everywhere. The UK was exploding with trans awareness, but with a very limited idea of what that was: white, Western, able-bodied, heterosexual. In other words, one that resembled me and my companions from Tumblr and other corners of the internet not one little bit.

Alongside this desire was a lot of self-discovery that felt very hard to share. So we waited until we were absolutely certain that it was the right time, and that I would be protected and emotionally safe within the performance.

> **EMMA** I think what I really valued about working with you in that period of time was recognising what was the art and what was life. And there was loads of life stuff. But for all that *None of Us is Yet a Robot* as a body of work shares a lot, there's a lot that's not in there, because it doesn't need to be, it informs who I am but doesn't need to literally be in the work.

The first public performance of *Language* took place at Buzzcut Festival in Glasgow. Many of the elements that became the final show were all there, but everything was in miniature. I was avoiding the audience's gaze, working on a table and using a projector to display small actions behind me on the wall. At one point I was joined onstage by my friend Felix Lane, of Open Barbers. Felix was one of the first trans people I met in real life, when I'd arrived for a haircut at Open Barbers several years previously. The concept of Open Barbers is simple: you get the cut you ask for – no judgements. Felix was instrumental in the forming of my understanding of trans politics, and a comment of his ended up as the final words of *Language*: in a moment of frustration, I had said: 'I just want to be treated like a woman.' Felix gently challenged what I meant by 'like a woman.' Treated badly? Rather than asking to be treated like 'a man' or 'a woman' – reinforcing some sort of universal binary – we should ask to be treated with kindness and respect. It's a principle I try to live by.

During that early performance, Felix and I both stood on stools while 'Natural Woman' played, pulled off our trousers and attempted to hold ten pence pieces between our calves and knees and thighs, to see if either of us could achieve the supposed perfect female shape. Of course neither of us could – it was just an example of toxic cis-normative beauty standards that are impossible to achieve whatever your gender identity.

**EMMA** We were calling it *Small Things* and after that first outing in Buzzcut was where we went, 'This is the wrong impulse, to hide away and be small and tiny.'

**RACHEL** The show expanded and the punk aesthetic crept back in – I think it was probably there all along – but just announced itself as not to be ignored, I think.

**EMMA** I think as well, I was finding who I am as a woman, and what my style is, and finally finding a bunch of queer punk-y trans women who were awesome and kind of like me, and you know, quite grumpy – but in a badass way! I'm too cheerful to be a punk! But finding that and it feeling really true in a way that the bowler hat and the cowboy boots and whatever else I'd tried had never felt right.

**RACHEL** You were just having a go!

**EMMA** I remember coming up to Bar Wotever with you one evening. That was a big deal. And now I'm like, 'What *was* the big deal?' I put eyeliner on and I wore some glittery socks.

**RACHEL** I laugh, but it's a big deal!

**EMMA** It's funny because it's socks and socks are silly! But also like, I don't wanna put down anyone who is experiencing that, because it is big. And I think there's actually something important in this sharing of all the excruciating embarrassing bits, and owning it rather than just talking about when it was cool and sorted.

The positive response to the first performance was cathartic and gave me confidence to be bolder – I didn't want to just be visible, I wanted to kick the fucking door down and nail my manifesto to the front of the building! We turned up the volume, literally, with my brother Keir Cooper (a genuine punk guitarist) joining me onstage. Instead of painting on a table, we stripped the back wall of the performance space and I spray-painted the words onto that. I was given a graffiti lesson in a Camberwell back garden, before putting my technique to fairly poor use with the rendition of a deliberately crass massive penis.

Literally and indelibly (until such time as they would be painted over) spraying these images and words to the walls of a theatre was an act of rebellion: in the same way as trans people often tattoo our skin, I was marking the building.

> **RACHEL** There was suddenly guitars, which hadn't been in Buzzcut! So there was that. That sounds like a small thing to say but it kind of wasn't. It was about voice, actually. I just remember the sense of 'fuck you' that you'd got by the time it opened at CPT, and the lights and the guitar, and that kind of – the journey to unapology.

> **EMMA** Do you remember we called the middle section 'Complex Trans Women'? Which is a phrase we picked up from somewhere and I remember us knowing what we meant, but not necessarily knowing how to actually articulate what some of the complications are to being a trans woman that [are] not present in the experience of being other flavours of trans person.

> **RACHEL** Yeah, I remember, it was a lot of work about transmisogyny and you were all like, 'Oh fuck me. This is complex. This is a shitstorm that I'm potentially heading into.'

> **EMMA** And I'm really proud that we attempted it – because I think what does set *Language* apart from some other work that I see, is that as much as it is for a cis audience and a trans 101, I don't think we round down, I think we attempted to get into the stuff that even now I don't know how to get into with people who are not experiencing it.

I don't think enough gets said about the attention that AMAB trans people get in the media and in the street, and how much of that attention is less about our identities and more about whether or not we are in possession of a penis. Most trans people have experienced complete strangers asking inappropriate, intimate questions about our bodies. Our medical and legal systems, too, are centred around this concern with our genitals. I have spent the past few years being frequently asked about it, by strangers and doctors alike. Many of the gatekeeping questions to access hormone treatment and other care have been framed around my penis – would I miss it? Is it problematic to me? Do I want to be 'the weird old woman with a penis?' (A direct quote from a senior medical practitioner.) This focus was looming large for me when I made *Language,* and has continued to be present in the work, connecting *Language* and *Hearty,* and highlighting how much *None of Us is Yet a Robot* has been not just about the language and political journey of trans awareness, but was, from the start, a somatic series of work about the trans body.

> **EMMA** It's interesting to see *Language* written down because it does feel dated. I can't really tell if it's because I've just moved on or times have moved on. I mean, a large part of *Language* was explaining what the word 'cis' means, because people didn't know of it. So that's definitely a dated thing. But I realise that this is not a piece that is meant for the trans community. This is a piece that is made to educate people who have less of a language of trans issues. And like we used to say, it's a trans 101, but hopefully went a bit beyond where other trans 101s go – by being a bit more factual or a bit more into the guts and the dirt of it than other things. But it was also written at a time when I was not experiencing the guts of it in the way that I do now.

> **RACHEL** It was tracking alongside a lot of first steps, I think. First steps of expression, first steps of declaration, first steps of medical stuff – all of those things were tracked through that process with me.

In some respects, *Language* feels young. Things have changed in an extremely short amount of time. It's another example of queer time: something that can be both young and old simultaneously. Only a handful of years have passed, and yet the landscape is completely, unexpectedly different.

> **EMMA** Someone recently was saying about ages in the trans community, and I guess the broader queer and LGBT community... When people are first coming out they have a lot of energy, but not necessarily as much wisdom!

**RACHEL** Being queer teenagers can come in your twenties, thirties, forties, and it comes with a mass of energy and a kind of blinkered and slightly delightful self-interest that is totally permissible, as it should be. But perhaps not the wisdom or the eloquence to express yourself. I think when I saw *Rituals for Change* I was like, 'Ah, okay, here we go. That's the art.' Or like, 'Here's the work that has a much bigger step away from the lived experience.' Those early works are necessary and important.

**EMMA** It's tempting to say, 'Just print *Rituals for Change*, that was the one that everyone liked.' But it's great that the other stuff is gonna be there to lead into it.

People have energy when they are fresh to the fight, and I think this is the kind of energy that informs *Language*. I was excited and passionate. And I was terrified.

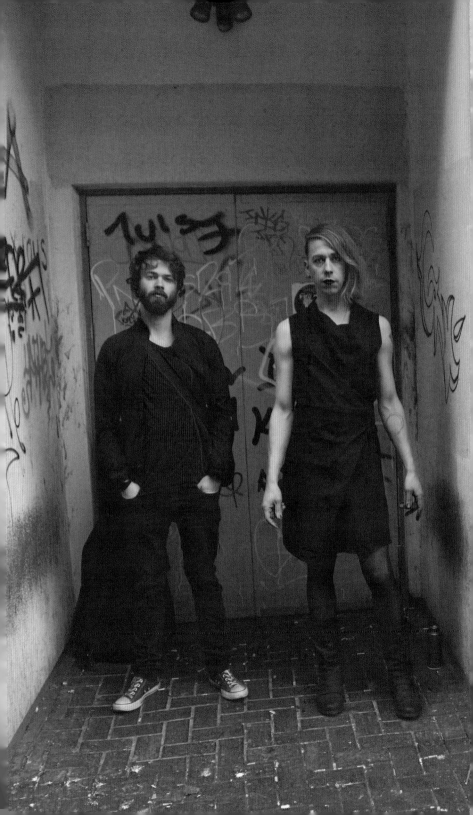

Pouring fuel oil onto the Blue Peter garden of gender,
this performance investigates why sometimes
it's necessary to smash things up.

**2012**

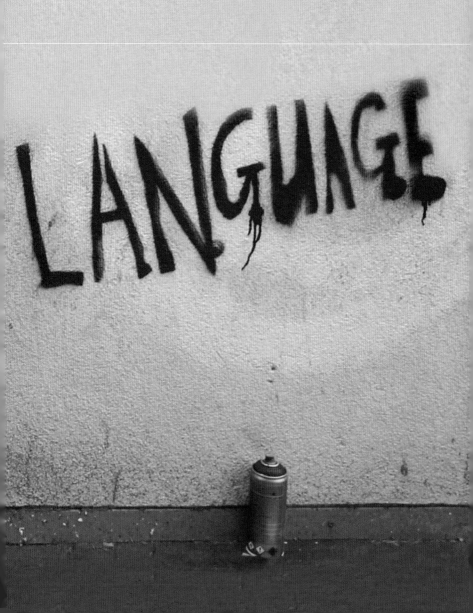

*A dubstep remix of a Blue Peter episode plays as the audience comes in. It is the episode where vandals broke into the Blue Peter garden. It is loud and hilarious.*

*There is a robot goldfish swimming in a glass bowl.*

*A punk guitarist is sometimes present.*

*The back wall of the performance space is exposed.*

*Emma sprays the Blue Peter logo on the back wall of the theatre space. She is wearing a black dress, orange boots and drinking from a can of beer.*

*Emma reads from a book – it is* Nevada *by Imogen Binnie.*

'Like, it would be nice to believe that you could just exist, just be some true, honest, essential self. But you only really get to have a true honest essential self if you're white, male, het, and able-bodied. Otherwise your body has all these connotations and you don't get the benefit of the doubt.'

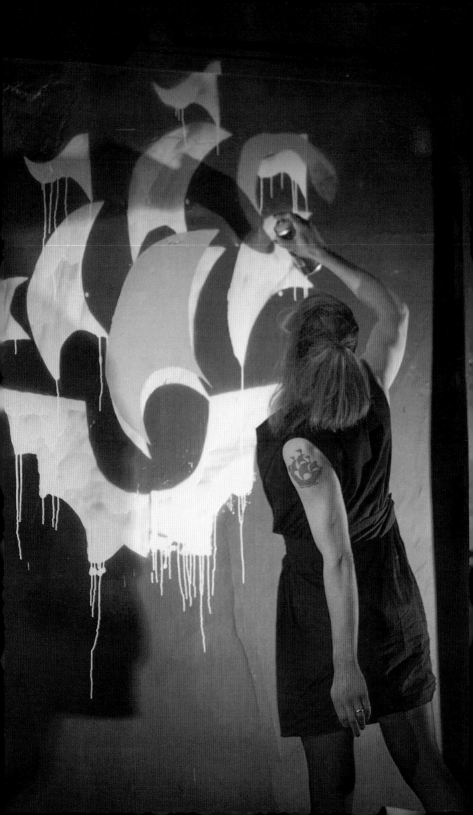

On the 21st November 1983, vandals broke into the *Blue Peter* garden and caused rather a lot of damage.

One really *cruel* thing they did was to pour fuel oil into the fish pond.

The vandals then broke a lovely ornamental urn given to the programme by Mr Taylor from Barnet. They then smashed up a sundial and then callously threw it into the pond.

And if that wasn't enough they then trampled on the bedding plants as well.

It's very sad to think that some people take such pleasure from harming their fellow human beings.

And from hurting animals as well.

I was actually on the programme the same episode – not because I was one of the vandals, nobody knew that about me yet – I was 4 years old and I was there because I had won my age group (under 7s) in a design-a-stamp competition – I was interviewed by Janet Ellis and met Peter Duncan, Simon Groom and Goldie the dog. The things I remember about the trip are the taxi ride home and meeting Brian Cant in the *Blue Peter* canteen. I don't remember an increased police presence, nor do I remember seeing any of the presenters crying or in visible distress due to the emotional trauma the vandals inflicted.

Nobody was being sick that I saw and I didn't witness any violent retaliations (or threats of the same) against the vandals.

**THEY POURED FUEL OIL INTO THE FISH POND**

**BROKE A LOVELY ORNAMENTAL URN**

**SMASHED UP A SUNDIAL**

**TRAMPLED ON THE BEDDING PLANTS**

**CAUSED A LOT OF DAMAGE**

*Music stops.*

I think that this was a big deal for my generation – it was the first time that something truly awful happened – the destruction of something sacred. It was one of those things you just don't do. I mean how could anyone vandalise the *Blue Peter* garden?!

The presenters and the viewers were all incredulous and Janet Ellis and Percy Thrower agreed that it could only have been done by people who were mentally ill.

# I AM A BLUE PETER BADGE HOLDER.

# I AM MENTALLY ILL.

# I AM A VANDAL.

*Loud music plays.*

*Emma spraypaints a massive spunking cock on the wall.*

*Music ends.*

I want to talk about gender and how I feel and about the ways in which we talk about our-selves and each other.

But there's a problem with the language.

Our language.

And that is that we don't have the words right now to have that conversation.

My stepmum had a book about calisthenics which described the ideal female body. It said that if you have a female body, you should be able to place three ten pence pieces between your ankles, shins and knees and keep them there, without them falling to the floor.

We are given plenty of examples of what it means to be a man or a woman.

We are told what men and women look like and this is constantly reaffirmed by the media, popular culture and the world around us.

by our parents.

ks about calisthenics

e Peter...

## ERE ARE RULES.

re we begin I want to **set out our terms** we are all on the same page.

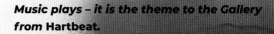

*Music plays – it is the theme to the Gallery from **Hartbeat**.*

*Emma spraypaints the words 'cis' and 'trans' on the wall.*

We all have a sense of our own individual gender.

We know – in our heads, or in our hearts or our bodies and souls – the way that we feel.

But not everyone's sense of gender is the same.

Simplistically (and immediately we are fucked) = the world could be broken down into people who are **transgender** and people who are **cisgender.**

When I say **cis** I mean somebody who does not identify as **trans**. Somebody for whom the gender they were assigned at birth matches the gender that they identify as.

This sense of cohesion between assigned and felt gender may be so in sync and so perfectly in balance that it is hard for the **cis** person to even conceive that it might be possible to feel otherwise.

That it is impossible to imagine what it feels like, if it isn't matching.

It is impossible to describe what it feels like using the words at our disposal.

**Cisgender** has its origins in the Latin prefix **cis**, meaning 'on this side of' – whereas the Latin prefix for **trans** means to span... Like a bridge...

'Vandal' has its origins in the Latin name for a town in Germany where the inhabitants liked to roam about and fuck shit up.

**I was assigned the gender male** ... **th based on the diagnosis of one doctor who verified my being in possession of a penis.**

I was assigned the gender female last year based on the diagnosis of six doctors who have verified my being in possession of *a clinically recognised and diagnosable condition, which is currently pathologised as a mental illness.*

**I am a transgender woman** because this past *(male)* doesn't contradict this present *(female)*.

I have had a traditionally acceptable male Western European lifestyle.

In fact as far as privilege goes, I was at the top of the easy tree as a...

White,

right-handed,

averagely sized,

mentally stable, able-bodied,

heterosexual,

healthy,

well-educated,

literate,

tall,

middle-class,

monogamous,

mid-thirties,

slim, self-defining,
urban-dwelling,

UK passport-holding...

MAN.

I'm a FATHER.

# I am your Dad.

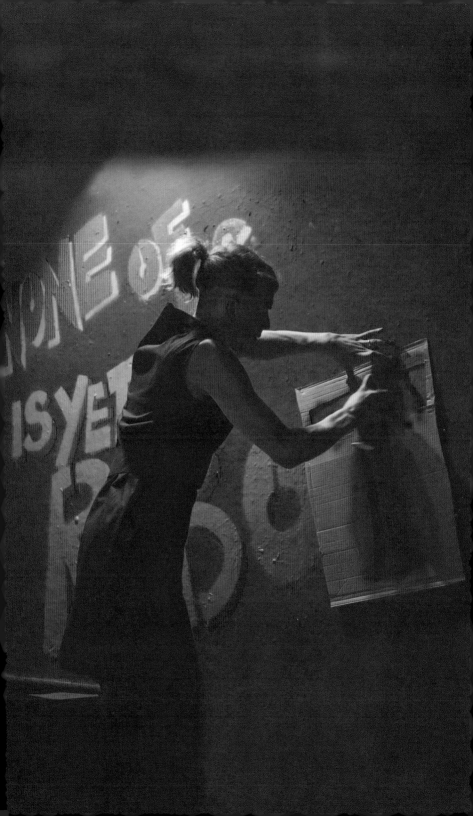

Out there I would like to be read and treated as a woman. But the world often reads and treats me as a man. Well not like a cisgender man, with the privilege. Not like before – more of a man that has something to hide... Well, a man with something wrong – a man that is trying to get away with something...

Mostly (at the moment) it's a look, a stare really... People look and then they look again and often they register their surprise... They are surprised and I imagine they feel that there has been some sort of deception that this woman is something I am wearing over the man... That there is some sort of cover up going on – instead of just being able to see that I am a woman who was assigned the gender male at birth because when that doctor looked he saw a penis and checked that box.

Out there I would like to be read and treated as a woman.

*Breathe – a rupture/a beat.*

No. Fuck that.

I would like to be treated with kindness and respect.

*Emma spraypaints the words for many different trans identities across the back wall.*

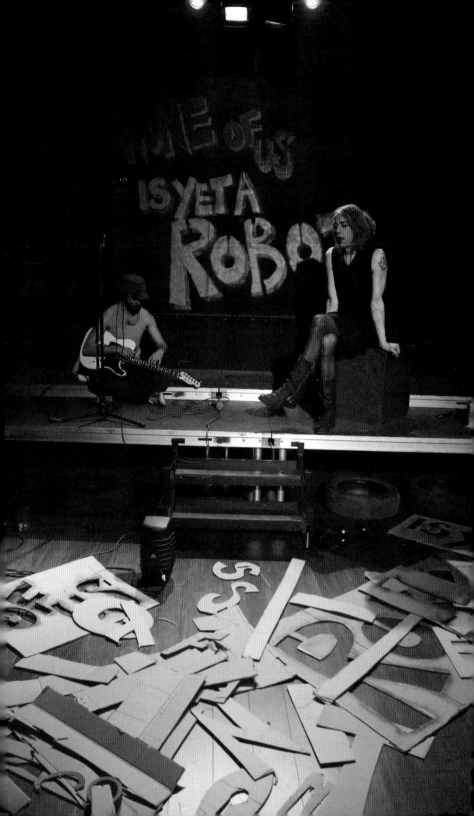

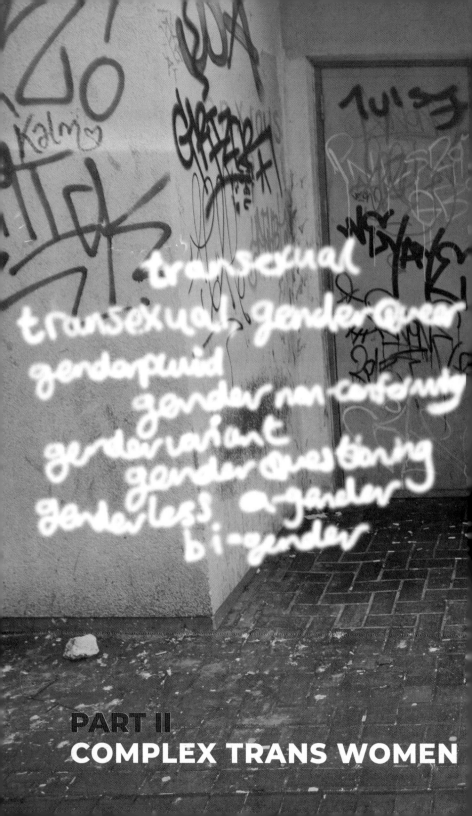

**PART II**
**COMPLEX TRANS WOMEN**

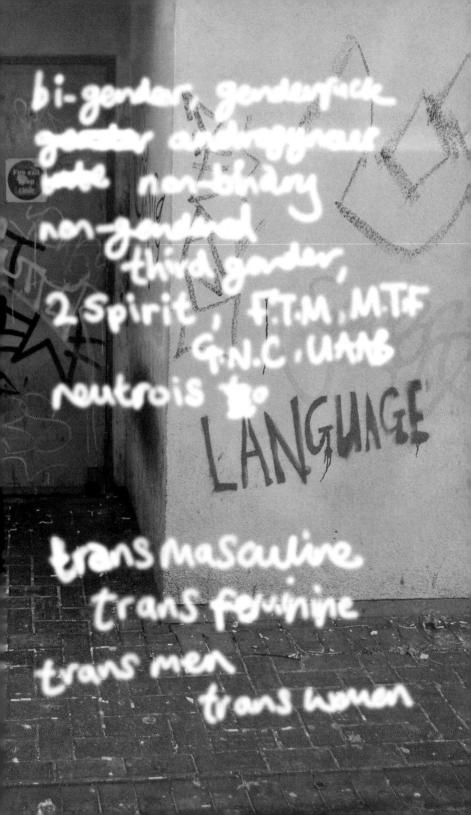

When I say **trans** the term is intended to include any and all non-cisgender gender identities.

I know that we like simple.

But the prefix **trans** does not simply mean crossing over from one side to another, like a bridge, but also 'going beyond'...to **trans**-cend.

The only criteria for defining yourself as transgender is to define yourself as transgender.

When I say that I am transgender I want to say that I don't feel that the male gender that I was assigned at birth matches the female gender that I feel.

What I want to say is that I am a trans woman.

Or in other words, a woman.

But I find it hard to say that because it is problematic.

Because there are people in positions of power who police the language, who would like to debate what I am allowed to be. Who say that I am inflicting an extraordinary act of violence. That I am not a 'biological' woman.

We are all biological – everyone and everything on this planet is biological – that your biology travelled a different route to mine doesn't make it any less natural, doesn't make it a fake. None of us is yet a robot.

So. First of all. Let us set out our

# TERMS.

Again.

*Music plays, beatboxing.*

*Into the mic:*

I am white and able-bodied and mentally stable and I have sat atop the privilege tree on a particularly comfortable branch. It is not easy to exist in any of these identities. It is not easy to ask the world to see anything outside the binary of man and woman that we are used to. It is even harder for those who do not sit on comfortable branches of the priviledge tree.

And yet. We look at this term – trans woman – differently. We look at all of them differently when they are on the body of someone perceived or presumed to have been assigned male at birth.

And that is because of misogyny.

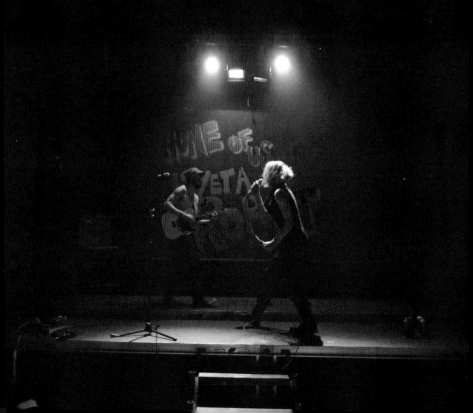

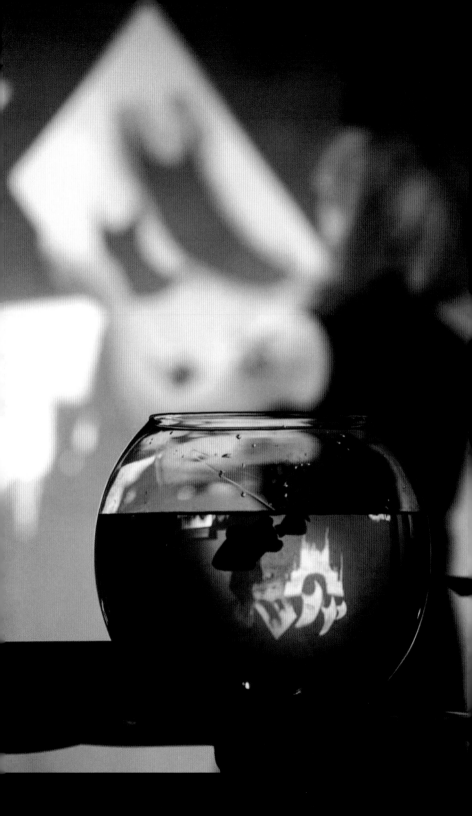

My name is Emma and I use female pronouns. I am asking the world to call me a woman.

This opens up problems.

All the shit.

Because **WHY WOULD ANYONE WANT TO BE A WOMAN?** We understand why those poor women would want to step up and claim some male privilege because we know that the system is fucked, but to resign your privilege of your own free will is suspect.

But us freaky trans women are disturbing because we suggest it is a valid choice to be a woman – not a fault of biology or a position to be sympathised – but an actual step up.

*During this speech, Emma deliberately sprays paint into the fishbowl – turning the water pink and obscuring the fish.*

We are viewed with suspicion and violence because **WHY WOULD ANYONE WANT TO BE A WOMAN?** There must be an angle – we are viewed as perpetrators of violence – of potential violence. By standing here and existing I am told that I potentially offer a threat. And so when I sit on the bus I feel I offer a threat to the innocent bystanders around me – the poor natural men and women who could be violently affected by my very presence.

At the time in my life when the world offers me a very real threat of physical violence I am told that I offer violence inherently.

Because of my being in possession of a penis.

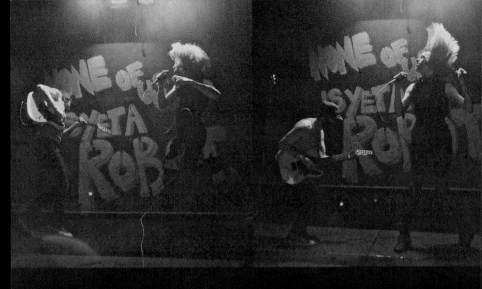

### Song.

If you're in possession of then you are not allowed
To be in possession of
You are not

## ALLOWED

If you're in possession of then you are not allowed
To be in possession of
You are not

## ALLOWED

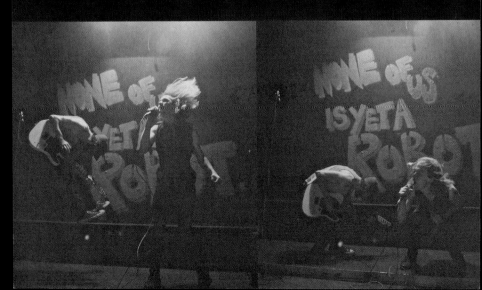

If you are in possession of a penis (and it is attached to your body) then you are not allowed to be in possession of breasts.

If you are in possession of a penis you may have a beard but if you are in possession of breasts you are not allowed to be in possession of...

...a beard.

If you're in possession of – woah-oh-oh-ohhhh
If you're in possession of – woah-oh-oh-ohhhh

If you are in possession of a penis you are not allowed

| to be in possession of | a fabulous haircut |
| to be in possession of | a smooth hairless body |
| to be in possession of | having sensitivity |
| to be in possession of | crying in public |
| to be in possession of | listening to other people |
| to be in possession of | intuitive parenting |
| to be in possession of | dependence |
| to be in possession of | gracefulness |
| to be in possession of | demonstrating weakness |
| to be in possession of | being sexually submissive |
| to be in possession of | E M O T I O N ! ! ! |
| to be in possession of | complexity |

If you're in possession of – woah-oh-oh-ohhhh
If you're in possession of – woah-oh-oh-ohhhh

If you are in possession of a penis you are not
allowed to be:

Long hair / GRACEFUL / smooth or emotional,

Caring /

Crying /

Flirting / listening / nurturing

Soft / tits / hips / lips / complex / lipsticks

Soft / tits / hips / lips / complex / no dicks

If. you. own. a penis. you

cannot.

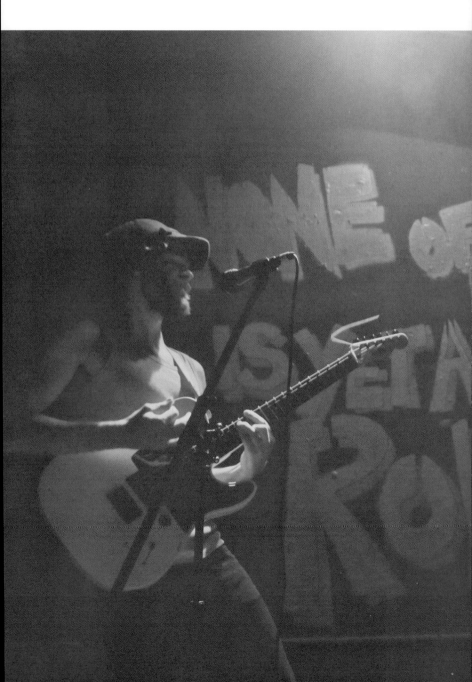

**IF YOU ARE OUT
ON THE STREETS
YOU ARE NOT ALLOWED
TO BE IN POSSESSION
OF A SPRAY CAN
OR A CAN OF FUEL OIL
OR A SMASHED SUNDIAL.
A VANDAL IS SOMEONE
WHO CAUSES DAMAGE
OR CHANGE TO A
PROPERTY THAT DOES
NOT BELONG TO THEM.
ALTERING SOMETHING
THAT PEOPLE VALUE
IN ITS ORIGINAL FORM.
SOMEONE WHO FUCKS
SHIT UP...**

# PART III
# ALL THE SHIT

*On the mic on the stand:*

The most common response to discovering someone is a trans woman in films and on television is for the character to vomit or to commit violence on her or just laugh.

In real life a common response to discovering that someone is a trans woman is to commit violence on her or laugh.

The most common form of defence used by somebody who has murdered a trans person is the trans panic defence – this is where you murder me and then say you did so because you were so surprised to find out that when I was born the birth certificate said penis that you **just had to murder me** and then your sentence is reduced.

The average life expectancy of a trans woman is between 32 and 34, depending on which statistic you use. I mean – that's not my life expectancy. With all this privilege.

But it's different if I leave the UK. Or when I go outside of London.

*'Natural Woman' begins to play under the text.*

Trans women are under suspicion because...
**WHY WOULD ANYONE WANT TO BE A WOMAN?**

With all this privilege...

Oh! You want to have sex with men but you are ashamed to be gay?!

Oh! You want to trick your way into women-only spaces and rape people?

Oh, it's just about the clothes?

Oh, you must be hilarious!

No. It just is...

But we tell a story that is 'I couldn't live any other way' to justify our decision. I tell **6** different medical practitioners that there was no alternative which is a lie – the alternative was fine.

# I SAY THAT THIS IS BETTER.

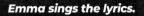

*Emma sings the lyrics.*

'Cause you make me feel

You make me feel

You make me feel like a natural woman

*Emma speaks over the music as it ends:*

I wake up and look in the mirror and I see a
natural person but that doesn't feel right and
so I do things that make that person less natural but then her reflection feels right and then
I feel that I don't know how to defend that
shape out there in the world and so I feel my
breathing get shallow and my heart races and I
find a million distractions to keep me from the
door and then I get out and I want to run back
and take it all off because how can it be real?

I want to talk about gender and how I feel and about the ways in which we all fuck each other up quite a lot.

But there's a problem with the language.

Our language.

And that is that we don't have the words right now to have that conversation.

Simply.

And I know we like simple.

It's really hard to articulate clearly with the language that we have at our disposal.

To articulate why sometimes before I leave the house I feel like I cannot breathe.

That I wake up and look in the mirror and I see a natural person but that doesn't feel right and so I do things that make that person less natural but then her reflection feels right and then I feel that I don't know how to defend that shape out there in the world and so I feel my breathing get shallow and my heart races and I find a million distractions to keep me from the door and then I get out and I want to run back and take it all off because how can it be real? And if I am questioning it's reality then how can anyone else fail to be violated by it.

Where can I stand so that I'm not perceived to be presenting a threat?

Where can I stand so I'm not threatened?

I don't have half an hour to try to explain all this when I'm waiting for the bus or taking my son to the playground.

I am altering this body – this female body in possession of a penis.

I am taking chemicals that send different messages to parts of my body containing instructions to vandalise what they discover.

I will be in possession of breasts and a penis.

I will be in possession of a beard and a smooth body.

I will be in possession of 35 years of white male privilege.

I will be in possession of a constant threat of violence and ridicule.

I will be in possession of confusion

of being a Dad
of waving to my neighbour
of smiling at your child on the bus
of shopping at Lidl
of going swimming
of using the toilet
of living my life
of doing everyday shit
of not crossing over but going beyond.

At the end of the programme segment, the *Blue Peter* presenters called the army in and together they worked hard to repair the damage to the garden.

The pond was drained and it was possible to rescue some of the fish but a few of them died.

The ornamental urn was glued back together but the cracks are still visible.

The flower beds were replanted.

But the garden was **never the same again**.

Because once you have taken something apart

the possibilities have expanded.

And to put it back to its original form

is only one of its many possible states.

*Emma pastes up over the graffiti a huge paper that says 'KINDNESS AND RESPECT'.*
*End.*

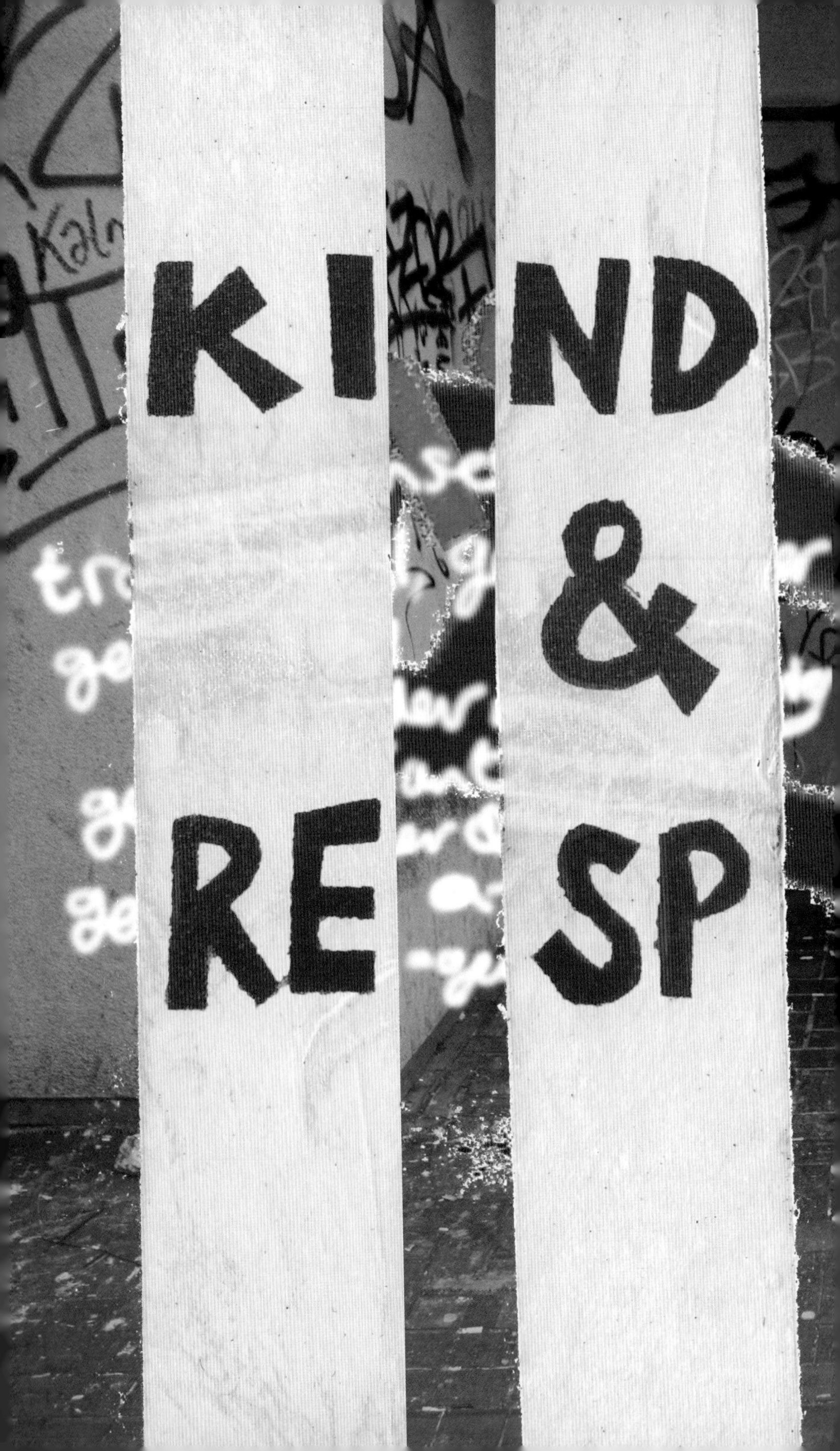
KI ND
&
RE SP

NE SS

EC T

# Doodle

In conversation with Maddy Costa, November 2018
Performance text: Forest Fringe, August 2015

'It still feels shocking to be a visible trans person. If you're a trans woman – well I speak for myself, I AM a trans woman – I'm always visible to a greater and lesser extent, depending on where I am.'

*Doodle* was originally made to fit Buzzcut Festival's 'Five Minutes to Move Me' format, where short intimate performances for a single audience member would take place in the cafe at the Pearce Institute, Govan. It was lovely to watch, each day of the festival, a different approach and a different artist – I remember Aby Watson dancing with an audience member to a record player, someone else composing with a typewriter. You could either participate and sit with the artist as a chair became free, or you could observe from a distance, with a cup of tea and a plate of food, something happening in the centre of a community space.

So the original format was me, sat at a table with a long roll of paper and a bunch of Sharpies, prepared to have a conversation about gender identity which I would illustrate and annotate with doodles – leaving a record behind. At this time I was already constantly answering questions... When you are trans there is an expectation that you will be willing (even grateful) to answer questions or 'debate' your identity. Always with an understanding that it is the trans person's duty to convince or change the cis person's opinion. It is a big responsibility, and it is exhausting – especially when you are just coming out and perhaps less empowered to say no. *Doodle* was an attempt to confront all this head-on.

**EMMA** I don't think it's the job of every trans person. I don't think that should come with the territory for every person who's othered. But I think it's the job of the performance artist. Not necessarily of the visual artist, or the writer. But part of what we do is we put ourselves in front of people. It's so simplistic, but part of the reason of that is to allow people to have a dialogue, or to change, or to see. I feel like I've been the first trans person a lot of people have met. And I have had a lot of conversations. Well, like you were saying, this... What did you say before about the way that we talked – there was care?

**MADDY** Care, yeah. Yeah. Taking care.

**EMMA** I think, again, I don't think I allow people to... I don't tolerate views that I disagree with. But I think I'm quite able to have that conversation, like you say, calmly and with care. I've done that with a lot of people over the last few years. I do feel like that's part of the job. I like that the work can speak in both directions. I do feel that *Hearty*, which is still being finished, and being shaped, is a spikier piece in general. That's because I feel a bit spikier now. I feel under attack in a way that I didn't feel under attack then. That's changed the nature of things. But certainly back with *Doodle*, it was very much about being there for people.

This first performance was terrifying. I had only publicly come out as trans the day before, and to be part of a performance festival where lots of people knew my past work was a challenge. I sat at my small table, listening to my (old) name being announced, and the first person to come over to me was theatre critic and writer Lyn Gardner. She immediately sat opposite me and said, 'Right then, what's this all about?' My stomach lurched. I had been having similar conversations privately – one-on-one interventions with friends and family about being trans – so the format was familiar. I unfolded myself to Lyn, who was incredible. We had a very nuanced conversation which I recorded as a doodle, and which continued to unfold over the following years. The same happened with Maddy Costa.

**MADDY** I really hold conversations that you and I had as kind of a model for a space where it's possible for people to talk about something that's really difficult, and work something out together. Those conversations kind of introduced me to a whole bunch of new stuff that I hadn't been thinking about at all. There's something really useful about the unfolding... Every bit of conversation opens up a new area that needs conversation.

It's a perfect illustration of where I was in my transition at this point – I had yet to start hormone treatment and was only just beginning to change my pronouns, or think about changing my name. Every day I had to explain myself to the people I loved and, increasingly, people I had only just met.

*'Sorry to email out of the blue, but there are some things going on for me right now and I am slowly beginning to spread the word and figuring out a good way of doing so. Sorry for not being able to say it face to face, but it's been a long time coming and I am excited to be able to finally share it.*

*The thing is. I am transgender.*

*And I am doing something about it. It is something that has always been the case, though I have only really been able to give it a name over the last six or so years and the past few years have been a lot of learning and thinking and planning and gradually coming further and further out.'*

There is so much admin to coming out; the extra labour of emailing people – work colleagues, friends, family – and explaining myself, then waiting for a reply (which may or may not be friendly), then providing support and information and reassurance for their fears. This is on top of official logistics such as changing bank details, passport, driving licence, utilities; and it all is completely separate to the medical appointments, the new negotiations of physical space, as well as the general day-to-day living of my life.

> **EMMA** Something that I think is a success for this piece is that it really responds to the people that I'm talking to. And it becomes exhausting as the performer of it, as the artist within it. Because you think, 'Oh, great. I'm having this conversation.' And then two minutes later, 'Agh! Someone else is here and I've got to shift my thing now.' Then, 'Oh, I've got this person here.'

> **MADDY** You have to be totally attentive all the time.

> **EMMA** You've really got to attend, as well as let half your brain be like, 'What am I writing up on this wall?!' Yeah, a piece that can totally shift and be like, 'Oh, okay. So you're here and what do you have to say?'

As with *Language*, my evaluation of this first performance was that the scale was wrong. Sitting quietly tucked away wasn't bold enough. The intimacy of it started to feel exclusionary, too – it felt invasive for onlookers to come over and look at the drawings, hard for them to know where to join in. As my confidence and my political indignation grew in tandem, I wanted the performances to be interventions; to disrupt a space rather than blend in. With *Language*, this became an increase in volume and disobedience. With *Doodle*, it was about scale and duration.

> **EMMA** I remember just setting up with my big blank wall in Forest Fringe. The idea being that it was gonna be big and in the middle of a space, so it was much more accessible for people to come and talk, but still the format being that it's me drawing. It's not a blank wall where everyone comes and draws, because when we've tried that it just becomes kind of chaotic. I wanted there to be more of a focus.

> **MADDY** Because it puts you in charge of the narrative that emerges, which I think is quite important in that scenario.

> **EMMA** Yeah. I think it's important that we acknowledge it as an art piece of which I'm the artist. Because I think that's something that I wrestle with. I remember at one point scrubbing out a thing, and writing, 'Is it free speech because I have the pen?' And that really coming up quite strongly. But it's not, it's an art piece. It's an Emma Frankland art piece, and that's fine.

For the next iteration – at Forest Fringe the same year – we used giant foam boards and covered a huge wall at the Out of the Blue Gallery. We were again situated in a cafe area, because it felt important that *Doodle* remain visible, taking up space in a public environment. The impact and participation had a broader reach than just the people who engaged one-on-one with a conversation. Before the performance I had a practice session with Isolde Godfrey, who gave me some really helpful pointers and practical advice regarding pens and drawing materials. Her tips, encouragement and techniques were invaluable in taking *Doodle* to a much larger scale – making it a complete performance instead of something unstructured.

Throughout *Doodle*, and throughout this project, I have been growing my practice to be a combination of performance and visual art – in *Language* this was graffiti art; in *Hearty* painted billboard slogans; in *Rituals for Change*, ceramics; and in *e g g / b o x,* illustration. I can make a mark if it is on the body; mould clay if it becomes a living thing... Draw, if it becomes a conversation.

I have since performed *Doodle* in a number of locations and circumstances, always beginning with a open question. It's been really exciting to ask questions not explicitly focused on trans or LGBTQ+ issues. *Doodle* is attractive, contained and interactive; an accessible way for people to disrupt a public space.

> **EMMA** I liked doing the Dialogue Festival *Doodle*, because the focus of it wasn't trans stuff. And it's been booked a few times by a college in Oxford, Wadham, who are kind of the queer college – if you're anything other, you go to Wadham. They have a great LGBTQ Awareness Week and stuff. They booked it. Then they booked me again for their Mental Health Awareness Week. And something that's so successful with *Doodle* is that it began very much as this way to be a visible trans woman who can answer questions about trans things, because that's what was coming up. And actually to be able to be a visible trans woman who can stand there and it's not about being trans – that's been a real joy.

The reason *Doodle* became an art installation was about visibility and being available to answer questions. It's funny, because much of what I do now relates to the idea of #NotADebate. I am always open to having respectful, informed conversations, that can change hearts and minds and provide learning on both sides. I'm just not debating people who are abusive and want to say trans women don't exist. But *Doodle* was made five years ago, before #NotADebate. On reflection, I was feeling so generous in terms of what I wanted to offer. *I will be visible and I will answer your questions* – that was the context for *Doodle*.

> **MADDY** I remember feeling like we were both coming at things from quite different places, and we were both... The phrase 'taking care' is really interesting because it has buried inside of it an idea of caution. It felt like a very incautious conversation, I feel like I don't have to be cautious with you. I think the kind of care that we're taking is care-free, and it's respect and not caution. It's exactly what you were saying about #NotADebate. Who ever wants to debate? I don't want to debate, but I do want to have conversations with people. How can art be a way of people having conversations? I still really believe the conversation does not stop when you walk out of the room and the work is kind of 'finished' in inverted commas. The conversation is also part of the work, as long as you're still having conversations that relate to an experience that you had in that room. *Doodle* is a work that will probably still be going on for the rest of my life.

> **EMMA** It's interesting, we talk about debate and dialogue. They feel like completely different things. One feels healthy in a way that the other –

> **MADDY** Yeah. There is no such thing as healthy debate. I'm pretty sure of it.

It is tempting to view the end result of *Doodle* as you would a painting, something that has a meaning that could be decoded... But it isn't. There is no cohesive whole, just a series of imprints and fossils of conversations and interactions in that space and at that time. Each *Doodle* imprint is as flawed and transient as the traces of clay and paint left behind after any of my other performances. The finished drawing doesn't represent the conversations, cannot hold their complexity and nuance; it simply shows that they existed, and that, for a moment, two people connected. Whether *Doodle* was in the context of an arts festival or Trans Pride, or some other public space, it was always about having constructive conversations that would ultimately bring people closer to understanding one another. I held all the pens, but I also crossed things out as my perception changed. This was not fine art. It was a doodle.

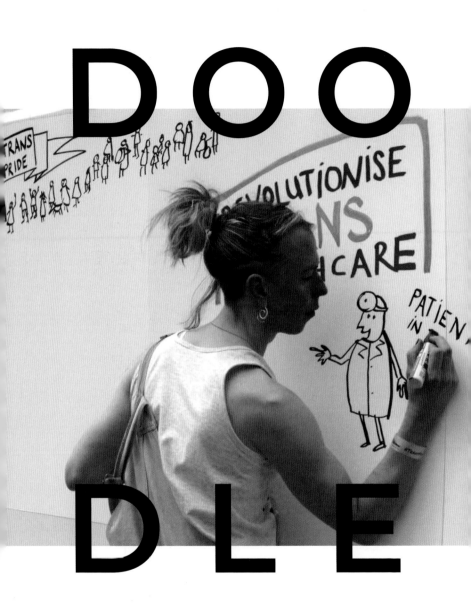

# DOO DLE

**A DURATIONAL LIVE DOODLING PERFORMANCE**

**2013**

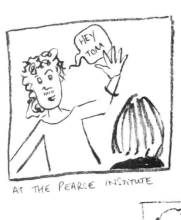
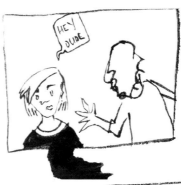

AT THE PEARCE INSTITUTE

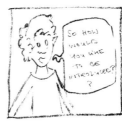
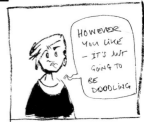

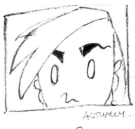
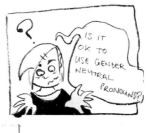

ACTUALLY...

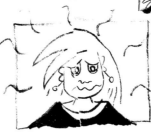

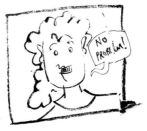
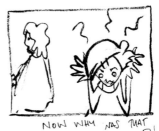

NOW WHY WAS THAT SO HARD?!

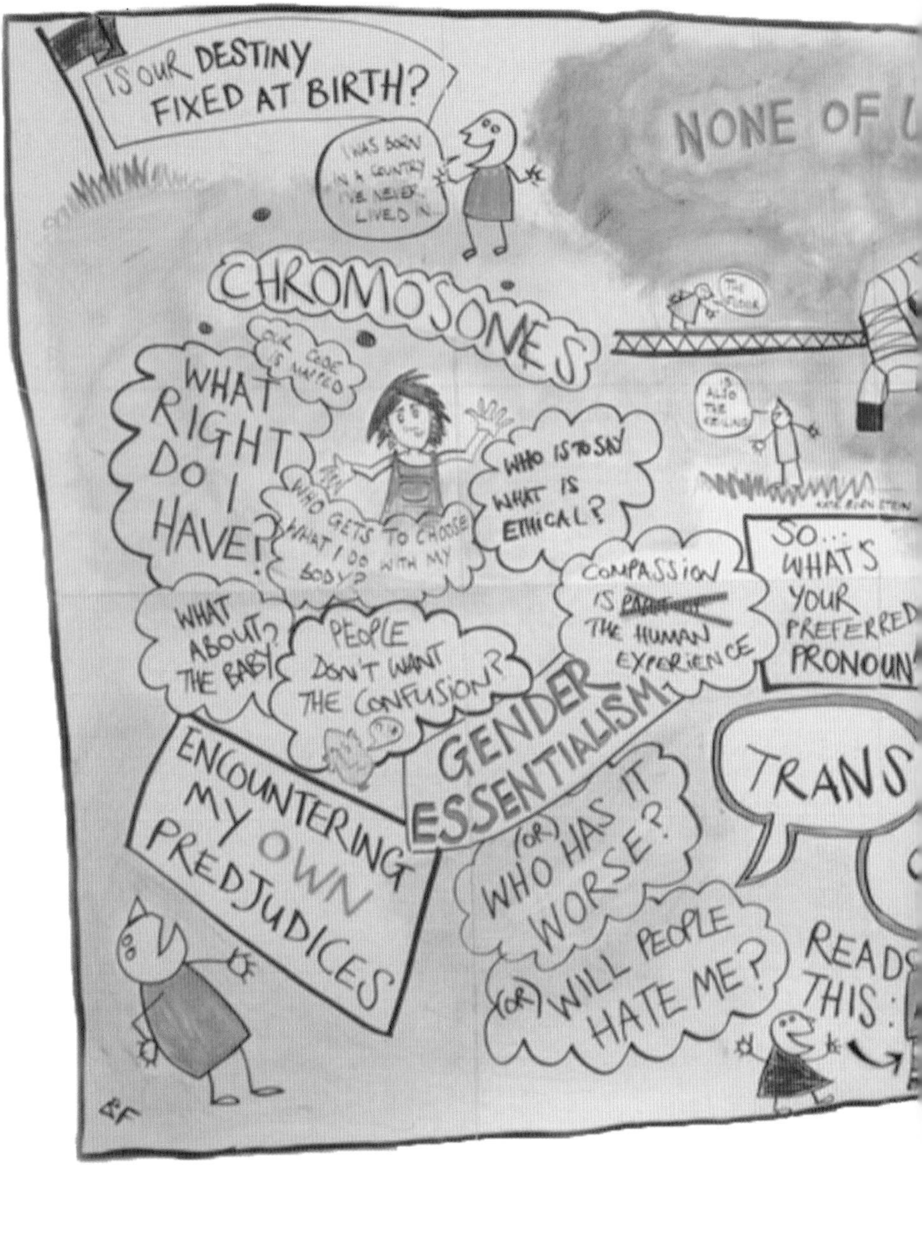
IS OUR DESTINY FIXED AT BIRTH?
I WAS BORN IN A COUNTRY I'VE NEVER LIVED IN
NONE OF
CHROMOSONES
WHAT RIGHT DO I HAVE?
WHO GETS TO CHOOSE WHAT I DO WITH MY BODY?
WHO IS TO SAY WHAT IS ETHICAL?
COMPASSION IS THE HUMAN EXPERIENCE
SO... WHAT'S YOUR PREFERRED PRONOUN
WHAT ABOUT THE BABY?
PEOPLE DON'T WANT THE CONFUSION?
GENDER ESSENTIALISM
ENCOUNTERING MY OWN PREDJUDICES
TRANS
(OR) WHO HAS IT WORSE?
(OR) WILL PEOPLE HATE ME?
READS THIS:

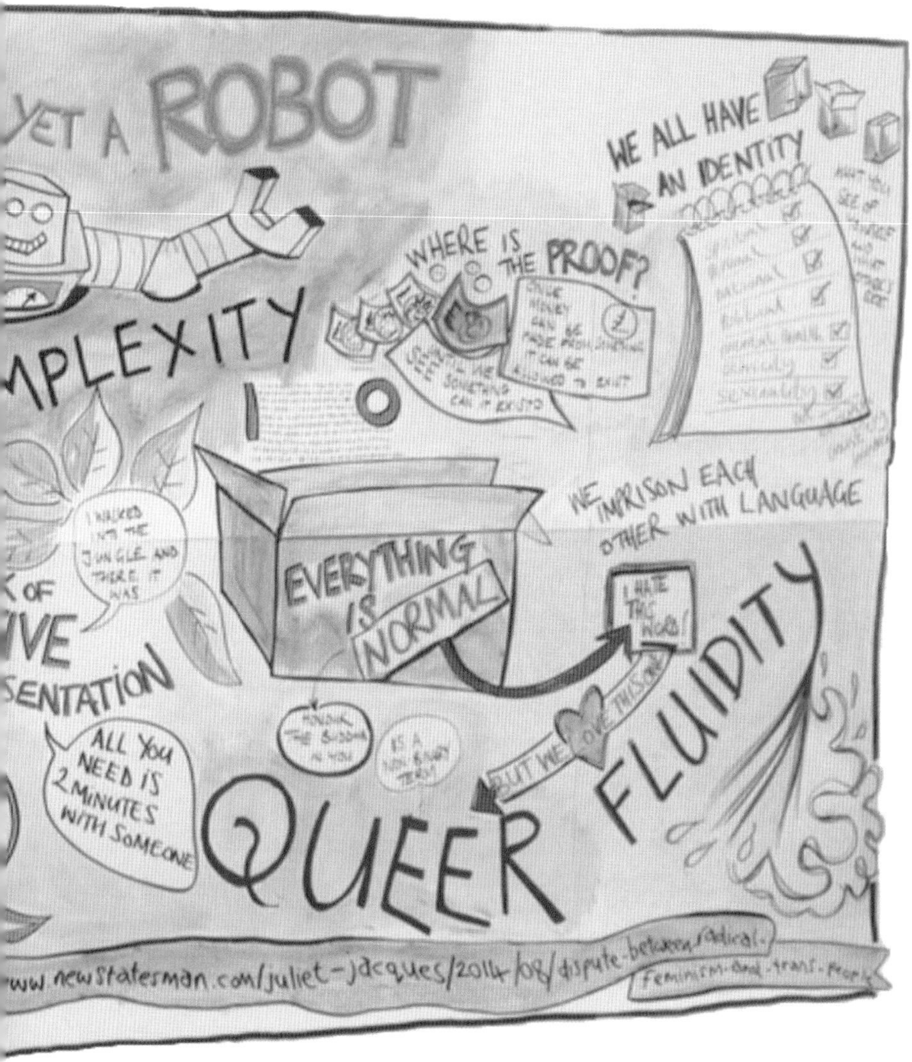
YET A ROBOT
WE ALL HAVE AN IDENTITY
WHERE IS THE PROOF?
MPLEXITY
I WALKED INTO THE JUNGLE AND THERE IT WAS
K OF
IVE
SENTATION
EVERYTHING IS NORMAL
WE IMPRISON EACH OTHER WITH LANGUAGE
I HATE THIS WORD!
BUT WE LOVE THIS ONE
FLUIDITY
ALL YOU NEED IS 2 MINUTES WITH SOMEONE
QUEER
www.newstatesman.com/juliet-jacques/2014/08/dispute-between-radical-feminism-and-trans-people

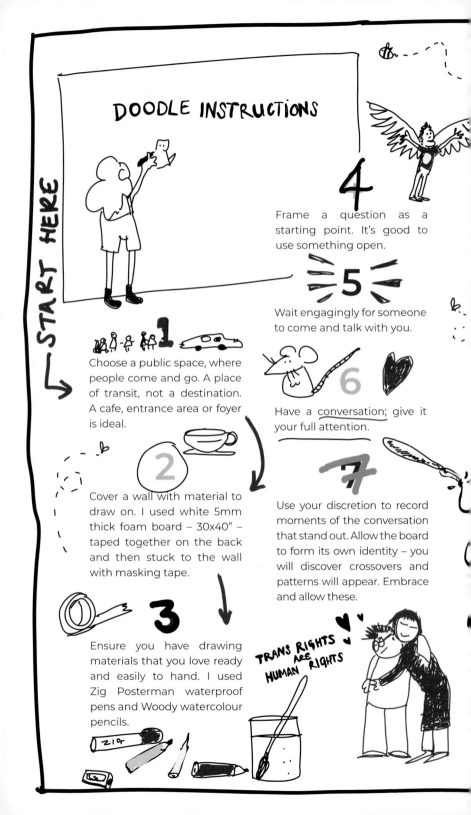

# DOODLE INSTRUCTIONS

START HERE

**1** Choose a public space, where people come and go. A place of transit, not a destination. A cafe, entrance area or foyer is ideal.

**2** Cover a wall with material to draw on. I used white 5mm thick foam board – 30x40" – taped together on the back and then stuck to the wall with masking tape.

**3** Ensure you have drawing materials that you love ready and easily to hand. I used Zig Posterman waterproof pens and Woody watercolour pencils.

**4** Frame a question as a starting point. It's good to use something open.

**5** Wait engagingly for someone to come and talk with you.

**6** Have a conversation; give it your full attention.

**7** Use your discretion to record moments of the conversation that stand out. Allow the board to form its own identity – you will discover crossovers and patterns will appear. Embrace and allow these.

TRANS RIGHTS ARE HUMAN RIGHTS

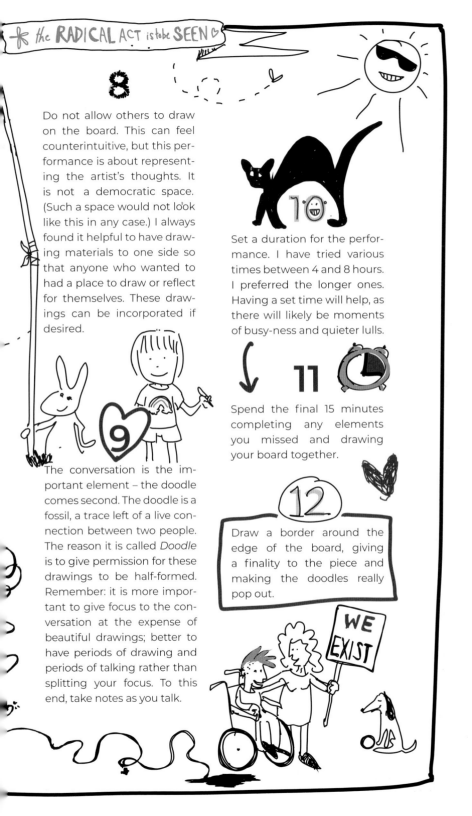

**8**

Do not allow others to draw on the board. This can feel counterintuitive, but this performance is about representing the artist's thoughts. It is not a democratic space. (Such a space would not look like this in any case.) I always found it helpful to have drawing materials to one side so that anyone who wanted to had a place to draw or reflect for themselves. These drawings can be incorporated if desired.

**9**

The conversation is the important element – the doodle comes second. The doodle is a fossil, a trace left of a live connection between two people. The reason it is called *Doodle* is to give permission for these drawings to be half-formed. Remember: it is more important to give focus to the conversation at the expense of beautiful drawings; better to have periods of drawing and periods of talking rather than splitting your focus. To this end, take notes as you talk.

**10**

Set a duration for the performance. I have tried various times between 4 and 8 hours. I preferred the longer ones. Having a set time will help, as there will likely be moments of busy-ness and quieter lulls.

**11**

Spend the final 15 minutes completing any elements you missed and drawing your board together.

**12**

Draw a border around the edge of the board, giving a finality to the piece and making the doodles really pop out.

HERE IS A BLANK SPACE FOR YOU TO MAKE YOUR OWN DOODLE!

# e g g / b o x
In conversation with Rosana Cade, December 2018
Performance text: Buzzcut Festival, March 2015

> 'And also it's fucking true. We are all
> fundamentally made of stardust and we are
> fundamentally related to sea anemones! Like,
> what?! Like, how is anything else an issue?'

When I called this show *e g g / b o x*, I didn't know how accurate
that was – that a term of affection for trans people beginning to
transition is 'egg.' I was an egg making a show about eggs, but
I didn't know!

It began development inside a tiny orange tent on an artist's
retreat in Cornwall, and was first performed later in 2014 at
Forest Fringe. I brought it to Buzzcut Festival in Glasgow the
following year, which felt significant after I had effectively come
out there via *Language*.

> **ROSANA** You coming and sharing that work with
> us is one of the things that I feel really happy about
> when I think about Buzzcut. I remember you
> applying the first year and articulating you were at
> the beginning of this transition process and that's
> what the work was dealing with, and I don't know if
> you necessarily said there was an element of coming
> out within it, but we could tell it was very early on.
> And then I remember you applying the second year
> and you were calling yourself Emma – I mean it was
> a new email address and everything and so it was
> like, noticing that step and feeling really just pleased
> to see that your journey was taking place and that
> we were a part of that.

It's surprising to remember that in the UK, back then, the visibility
of trans and gender non-conforming artists was significantly
less than it is now, even within a progressive fringe space like
Buzzcut – which specifically explores performance on the margins
of live art and theatre. But gender variance was not a topic that was

broadly represented; even now, it's hard to recognise that trans artists, and trans people, are very much a minority, despite the widespread fearmongering that we are expanding out of control.

**ROSANA** [Because] Buzzcut was an open application platform, we wanted to be there for artists to use in a way that was good for them. And often we think of that in terms of people's careers – but we always felt like it could be something more than that as well, because the atmosphere at the festival was hopefully one that people found very generous and open, just because of some of the structures that we put there. But we did really want it to be a place that people could, I suppose, take risks or go on personal processes, and I know a few artists who during it made work that was really quite transformational in lots of different senses. And I think your journey with that work was something that we were just so happy to have as part of the festival, and to be coming back each year and to see how you were expressing the changes that you were going on. And I think for me at the moment, being with Ivor [MacAskill] and us thinking about work that we might want to be making alongside his transition – it's so inspiring to have witnessed and been part of that journey that you went on.

**EMMA** I always found Buzzcut so positive and it definitely was all of the things you've just said you were hoping for. By the final year at Buzzcut there was tons of trans work, and artists identifying as trans and non-binary, and work looking at that, which wasn't the case in 2013. And you know, 2014 was the year of the Laverne Cox *TIME* Magazine cover, and coming out, and I guess it just feels strange to feel like – in the context of Buzzcut, which I always felt was so cutting-edge and at the really exciting part of international live art and Scottish live art and UK live art and theatre – that something like *Language* was articulating something that wasn't being put out there.

**ROSANA** I would definitely say that there was an increase in the last of two or three years of the festival where we were getting so many more queer artists applying, and those sorts of issues around gender being explored. And I remember maybe in the first or second year being like, 'Oh I really want to be programming queer work but we're not getting those applications!' Which feels really weird now, because I think actually the live art community in the UK has a lot of queer people who are programming things and it feels like there's just loads of really interesting queer artists, and I think Buzzcut by the end felt like a queer space even though we didn't necessarily call it that, and we were careful with what labels we would use for things because – you know, some labels that feel inclusive to some people might feel exclusive to others. I tell you who else was there, we had Open Barbers. I remember they came up that year as well and that was really brilliant, to make connections with them. But I think before that I didn't feel like there was a trans presence – it felt like a beginning of connecting with certain people within the trans community.

e g g / b o x was experienced by only one audience member at a time, who was invited to sit inside a giant cardboard box; I then performed the piece inside a second box. Onlookers would be unaware of the activity taking place inside – all they would see were two closed boxes. The show's form was inspired by a PechaKucha challenge (a method of presenting a slideshow which permits only a fixed time per slide – twenty slides with only twenty seconds each) that I was set by Rachel during rehearsals for *Language*; and by the book *Sex and the Nature of Things* by N.J. Berrill – a Canadian biologist writing in the 1950s. I found the book whilst performing in a musical tribute to *Ghostbusters* – I began pretending to read it onstage and was swiftly drawn in. *Sex and the Nature of Things* is remarkable. Where others were content to draw parallels between humans and apes, Berrill was finding connections between us and *all* life on the planet – from grass and sea cucumbers (which have the ability to change their gender) to single-cell eggs of every kind. This is probably just basic marine biology, but to me at the time – experiencing harassment and disapproval for my visible transgressions of gender norms –

a textbook that found a commonality between all living things felt hugely validating.

*e g g / b o x* was possibly a subconscious attempt at reconciliation. Looking at it today, I am almost embarrassed by its generosity to a cis spectator. It's a piece that says: 'We are all the same.' Subtextually, 'Please don't hate me.' But it's also a collage of words and music that I felt inspired by at the time. Quotes from books, blogs, and private conversations with other trans people. I used Berrill's beautiful chapter headings as prompts for the audience member or for myself.

As we were each inside the cardboard boxes, we were unable to see each other; it was a kind of hiding, but also a private space within which to grow. At a time where my appearance still dissatisfied me and triggered public reaction, I wanted a conversation with an audience that wasn't tainted by how they read me physically – that would allow me to explore something without feeling a pressure to be perfect.

> **ROSANA** I guess I feel that one of the values of art is that it can reveal complexity within experiences. And I suppose I think it's something that – you want to be positive about your experience of being trans because you want to seem sorted, but also because that feels really important in terms of trans positivity. There is this real desire for a lot of people to be very positive about trans experiences to show that you can be trans and you can be, you know, living a good life. But of course like all experiences that we go through [we] can feel lots of different things at different times, and it can be very very positive and at the same time have difficulty within it. And so I think to be able to – the act of making work that helps to speak to those different emotions or some of the challenges, and to be able to have that record of that, at the same time as being in a place to be able to look back, is really important.

> **EMMA** Travis Alabanza speaks about being seen as kind of a 'messy tranny.' I think about that so often and how representations of trans women or

transfeminine people are often – and again this is misogyny, it's not just the trans thing – but this pressure to always look good and to always look like I'm better off having transitioned. And that's huge pressure! And sometimes I think of that thing that Travis said, and I feel a real ability to own it. Like, if I don't want to shave, or if I put my make-up on really fucking thick, but I did it because I liked it that way and stuff like that – sometimes I feel that's kind of a protective thing, to go, 'Yeah I'm going to be messy today.' And yeah, that might make for difficult encounters, but I'm going to own it.

**ROSANA** I think messiness is really important. I'm just thinking about issues around minority representation. When it's so limited you have to be absolutely perfect to be the person who's representing that group. So if you're making a piece of art about a certain minority experience it has to be able to do everything, and it has to speak to everyone in that group. Even in terms of like, how we represent our bodies and – yeah, it's stressful.

For a performance that felt very sparse to the audience member, it was surprisingly technical. I used a visualiser to project live images inside the other box: my hands painting, or a low-fi lighting effect. We were also connected by a set of walkie-talkies and via an old-fashioned radio which sat in their box, which I controlled to broadcast a soundtrack into their space.

**ROSANA** There's something within the performance that had a sense of – it had technology within it but it also had a real DIY aesthetic at the same time. I'm not very technologically minded, so my mind is blown when I'm in a box and there's something being projected and like, I know it's coming from the other one but I don't know how. So it was really high-tech but also felt very DIY and low-tech... And it was in the cardboard box. So there was something that also speaks to a shifting scale, and something that as an experience is constantly shifting between being about the person in the domestic, to being something that's incredibly advanced that engages with very, very advanced technology.

Performing the show became a dance – or a ritual. Technically precise and with a large amount of physical activity, while the audience member sat in relative peace. Like transition, however, my fierce activity (dancing, painting, cueing sound and lighting effects) went unseen – the only point of connection being towards the end, when the boxes opened and we met.

I performed the fifteen-minute piece back to back over a period of four to six hours. A loop, revisiting each moment, each time with a slightly different outcome depending on the connection with the audience member. Sometimes we would sit in silence. Sometimes we would embrace. It echoed what was happening in my life at that time: repeated coming out conversations with friends and loved ones regarding my transition, which followed a rehearsed script but always had a different outcome.

> **ROSANA** One thing that I remember very strongly from the performance was the really joyful moment at the end, where – if I'm remembering it right – we both burst up out of the boxes, or like, I came up and I saw you and we were dancing and it just felt incredibly joyful. That's quite a strong memory.

> **EMMA** Yeah. Chapter 14, 'Dance, Wings and Song', and then we dance to 'Modern Girl' by Sleater-Kinney, which I love. That moment of dancing, and dancing without being seen. And then coming together, and that coming together was different. We may well have danced together and with other people we just held hands and looked at each other, and with other people we talked a lot. And so it was very unique to the other individual what actually happened when the boxes were opened. Which is something that was nice. And I think it's essential with one-on-one work, isn't it, that the presence of whoever the audience member is, whatever they bring to the piece necessarily alters that piece.

It feels really nice to sit inside a huge box and it is impossible not to feel like a child again. I had the boxes specially made, big enough that it was comfortable to sit inside and feel surprisingly cosy and safe. A place of refuge, away from the harshness of the world outside. *e g g / b o x* was another attempt at communicating the contradictions of transition: the joyfulness in the middle of the pain.

**ROSANA** I have this experience of my partner transitioning, which is now something I suppose I'm relating a lot of things to. We talk about it and it feels sometimes so huge and seismic and monumental and emotional, and then, sometimes, it feels very, very light and we recognise the constant change everywhere in everything, and this being one of those [things]. And it's not either of those things ever completely. It's so many different things and also I think there's something that is very, very personal about it. And then there's also – you know obviously I mean this is a really like cliché thing – but it is an intimate experience alongside a very medical experience.

**EMMA** I never was able to say, 'I'm going to become a trans woman and I'm going to have a medical transition.' Those things were absolutely inconceivable to me. What happened was I took these very incremental steps and very small things, but every one of those small things felt just so emotionally huge. And then by the time I got to the things that arguably are quite big, like beginning to take hormones or whatever, they felt more manageable and actually smaller in some respects. I mean at the moment I'm at the point of considering various surgical things and what-have-you, and I feel like – 'Oh, whatever, yeah maybe I'll do that. Maybe that's necessary.' Emotionally that feels like a smaller step than it did to go out in public wearing eyeliner, even though there's people who identify as male who were assigned male who go out and wear eyeliner because they're goths or whatever! So yeah I completely relate to that. And there was something playful about *e g g / b o x*, because it was happening inside a cardboard box, which is also a nice thing to do. We don't get to sit in cardboard boxes as adults.

**ROSANA** It definitely had this childlike quality to it that I really enjoyed as well. In some ways if we think about that there's real space for playfulness and naturally accepting lots of different ideas about how people might be when you're children and you're in that mode, and then obviously we –

in lots of cases people get more rigid as they learn. But I think something about that piece is – which seems like such a simple thing to say – this idea that everything is connected and humans are born as babies and then there's so much potential of what they might be open to accepting or experiencing. Maybe there's something in that childlike nature of it that helped it to feel like there was potential.

Many of the themes from these performances can be felt resonating in each other, and the presence of a cardboard box is also central to *Hearty*. Throughout the show, I ask the question: 'What could be inside?' In a very real way, perhaps what is inside is a younger me. Or a future trans woman. An egg, waiting to hatch and in need of support, love and celebration.

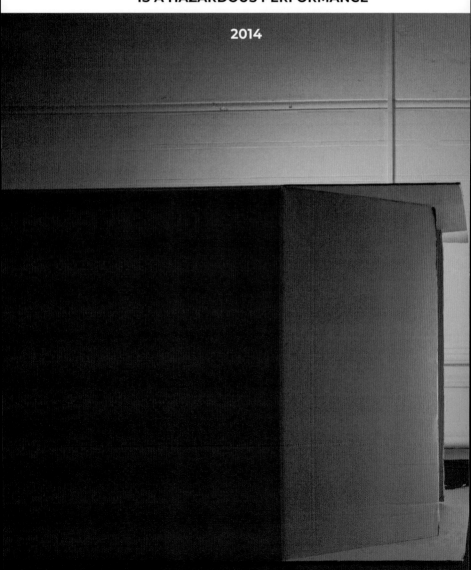

**GROWING FROM AN EGG
IS A HAZARDOUS PERFORMANCE**

2014

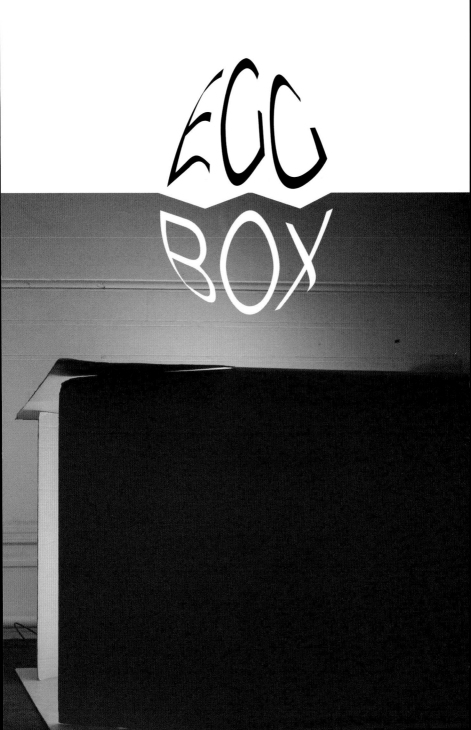

# PART ONE

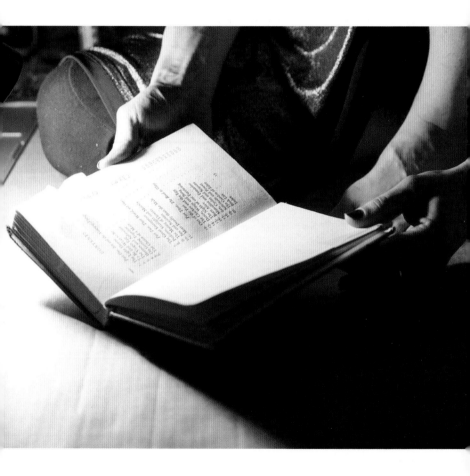

**SEX**          **AND THE NATURE OF THINGS**

*'Feeling Good' by Nina Simone plays on the radio.*
*The light dawns inside the box and there is an effect like a sunrise.*

## 1 – THE LIGHT DAWNS

**spoken:**
'We are creatures born of water, made mostly of water, living on dry land with only the gaseous air surrounding us, looking across the universe to distant stars.' (N.J. Berrill, *Sex and the Nature of Things*)

## 2 – TO BE AND WHAT TO BE

**text:**
'Sex is no longer a simple, clear-cut difference between the two kinds of individuals of a species. In human beings and many animals, the lines are smudged and it is a case of more or less – not either or.' (N.J. Berrill, *Sex and the Nature of Things*)

**spoken:**
A man has a deep voice and grows a moustache, but he has nipples too. The world grows complicated and so do we.

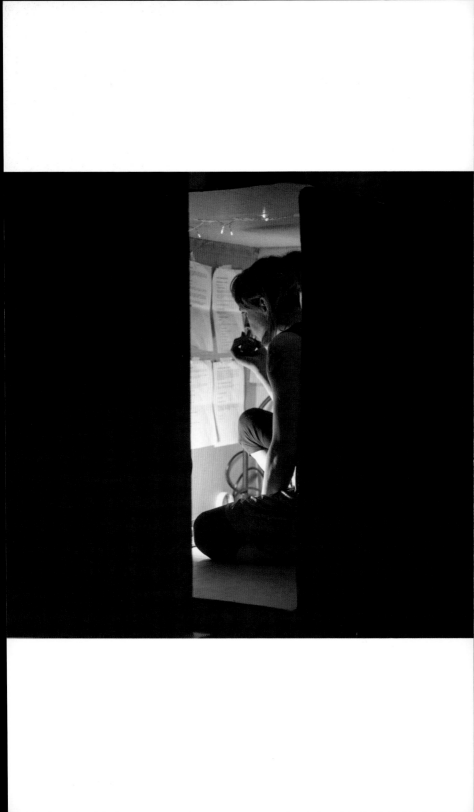

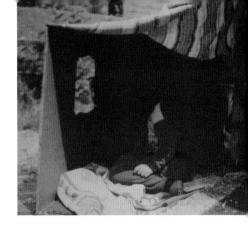

### 3 – THE VIRGIN EGG
*Emma draws an egg.*

**image:**
**Young Emma inside a box**

**spoken:** Sometimes the things that you can see are insignificant or wrong and sometimes the things you can't matter a great deal. Really, really big things can be so small that they are invisible, and really, really small things can have a massive impact.

### 4 – HERMES AND APHRODITES

**text:**
Once upon a time, we were all sea cucumbers.

### 5 – ON GETTING TOGETHER

**voiceover:**
'Hormones are chemical prostheses, political drugs. The substance not only modifies the filter through which we decode and recodify the world; it also radically modifies the body and, as a result, the mode under which we are decoded by others.'
(Paul B. Preciado, *Testo Junkie*)

## 6 – THE CHOICE OF A MATE

**image:**
**Hannibal and Gemini**

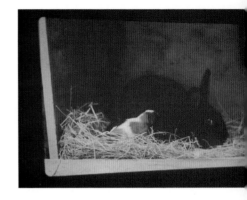

**spoken:**

This is a rabbit called Hannibal. Hannibal lived with a guinea pig called Gemini. Even though they were different nobody ever said this was weird.

Rabbits are what's known as prey animals. One of the distinctive things about prey animals is that they don't show pain on the outside. This means that they might be in distress or feel that something is wrong – but you wouldn't be able to tell by looking.

It is difficult to tell the sex of a rabbit by looking at a picture – unless perhaps you are another rabbit. This is because rabbits cannot grow moustaches.

# 7 – THE GREAT EMERGENCE

**video:**
**Egg hatching**

*'Mike Mills' by Air plays*
*on the radio.*

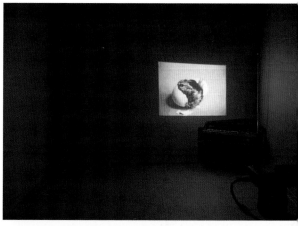

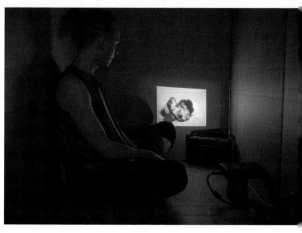

# PART TWO

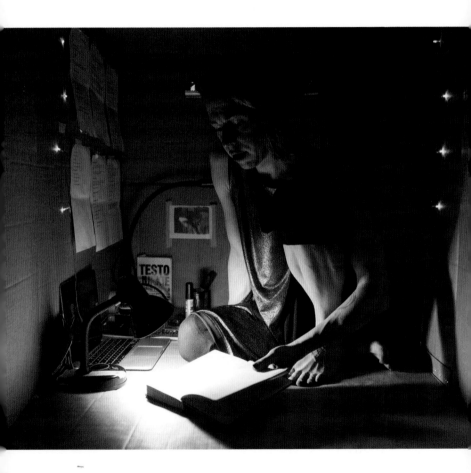

**THEIR WORLD,**                    **NOT OURS**

## 8 – PERFUME, STARLIGHT AND MELODY

**text:**
Breathe, see, hear.

## 9 – THE MATING OF FLOWERS

**spoken:**
'Endocrinology can be read as the biologisation of a theory of broadcasting, distribution and treatment of information.

A substance which has to be turned out into the blood at repeated intervals to produce in some distant organ or organs a physiological response proportional to the dose.

A biological postcard, a chemical telephone message, a long-distance biocall.' (Paul B. Preciado, *Testo Junkie*)

The world grows complicated and so do we.

## 10 – SEX AND SOCIETIES

**text:**
'Human society is complex and unstable – which makes living in it interesting, irritating and hopeful.' (N.J. Berrill, *Sex and the Nature of Things*)

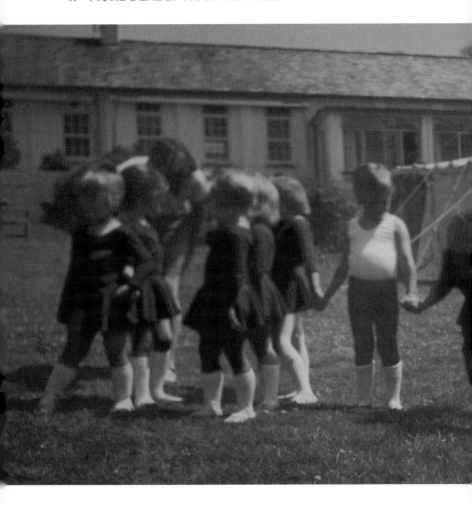

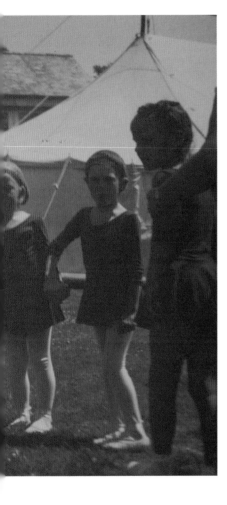

1 in 10 people in the world
are left-handed and 1 in 10
animals in the world is an ant

1 in 10 people prefer Pepsi

1 in 10 have had an out-of-
body experience

1 in 10 can't stay still

1 in 10 are no longer religious

1 in 10 are unafraid

1 in 10 eat, sleep and
drink without worrying

1 in 10 have breakdowns

1 in 10 die before their time

1 in 10 fight their destiny

1 in 10 can't swim

1 in 10 have had a
spiritual awakening

1 in 10 can't make their mind up

1 in 10 have doubts

1 in 10 go through with it

1 in 10 don't like what they see

1 in 10 don't cry anymore

1 in 10 want to make it all better

# PART THREE

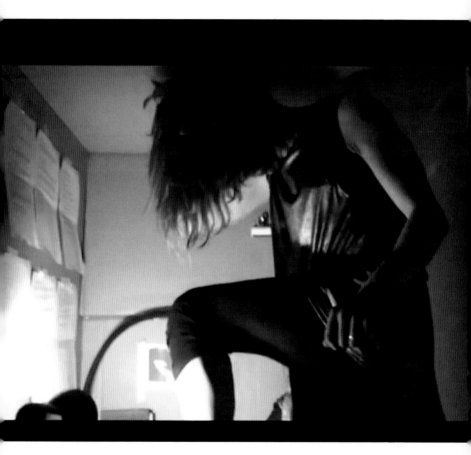

**THE ROAD**                    **TO GLORY**

**voiceover:**
'The thing about insisting on your identity, even vocally, is that the world doesn't see identity, doesn't make decisions about how to treat you based on it.

I'm frustrated by the ways we can't seem to talk about nuance around different kinds of experiences, different relationships to identity.' (Anonymous, online post)

## 12 – OUT OF THE PAST

**spoken:**
'I find it hard to comprehend, let alone convey, the magnitude of the event – the conquest of the land by watery creations that became transformed themselves during the process of their emergence.' (N.J. Berrill, *Sex and the Nature of Things*)

*'Modern Girl' by Sleater-Kinney plays on the radio.*

### 13 – THE CHICKEN AND THE EGG

*Emma draws cracks on the egg,*

### 14 – DANCE, WINGS AND SONG

**text:**
Let's dance.

*We dance in the boxes.*

### 15 – THE NIGHT OF OUR FOREBEING

**video:**
**A nature film from the 1970s**

*Meditation music plays on the radio.*

### 16 – BORN ALIVE

**text:**
It's time to leave...

*(At this point we opened our boxes and saw each other for the first time. I read the next piece from the book and then they read the one after...)*

## 17 – MASCULINE AND FEMININE
*Read aloud.*

**spoken:**

'We are human beings. We are also warm-bodied mammals with all the characteristics of our class; and we and the rest are quadruped with lizards and birds and frogs, no matter what use is made of our front pair of limbs. And all quadrupeds are also vertebrates, the backboned assembly that includes all fishes and even the Lamprey eels that scourge the Great Lakes and predate fish in time and structure. When we go beyond them, we land in the sea with the sea-squirts.' (N.J. Berrill, *Sex and the Nature of Things*)

## 18 – SEX, CYCLES AND SEASONS
*Read aloud.*

**spoken by audience member:**
'Growing from an egg is
a hazardous performance
and most of us are luckier
than we realise.' (N.J. Berrill,
*Sex and the Nature of Things*)

## 19 – SOLITUDE AND POWER

**spoken:**
Hello, I'm Emma...

*(And the audience
member responded...)*

## 20 – THE GARDEN OF EDEN

**voiceover:**
'My own feeling, or belief
if you prefer such an
immovable word, is that
the universe is one and its
wholeness is all-pervading.
I believe, with others, that
energy and matter, mind,
emotion and spirit are all
qualities of whatever this
universe is made of.'
(N.J. Berrill, *Sex and the
Nature of Things*)

*'Follow Your Arrow' by Kasey
Musgrave plays on the radio.*

**text:**
THE END

absolute. Sex ... must be at the bottom of it, but even here the power is relative and other factors enter in.

When the male sex hormone is injected into low-ranking hens they rise rapidly to the top of the order. There is an increase in general vigour and willingness to fight, and the ... is found and more or less respected by their fellows. This ... hormone produces this effect; what is injected is added to the ... which a male already has, for we need to remember that the ostrich-producing male as well as female hormones in any case. The male hormone becomes the hormone for aggressiveness, and given enough ... by man or nature, a bird of either sex becomes a bully. The female hormone merely increases female submissiveness and other similar traits.

Hormones are ... everything, either in birds or ... . Many a female bird has bettered her social position through male favouritism. A female ... law returned to colony after several months' absence and ... found a male ... himself cock of the rock—and ... as his mate a small, social nonentity. The next day, the lady took to bullying the former despot ... many others who had to ... she kept her in her place ... . In ... anachronistic situations can arise among birds as ... as human beings. The badge of office may be necessary to maintain a social order, but tyrants should always be tempted with a little caution ... ... this has been said before, but when hormones run out ... and power for power's sake becomes a ... displacement is no more than its just reward.

Too much of anything is always harmful, and I doubt that dominance in the world of nature is often carried to the excesses exhibited so freely among ourselves. One ... ... is generally balanced by another. It is surprising.

what a sudden flush of prolactin can do to a dominant male, although much of this is surmise based on what we know of hens and rats and aquarium fish. You can watch the antics of a tiger and interpret them in terms of glands, but you don't approach a tiger with a hypodermic syringe in your hand. Curiosity can go too far.

In any case, even a crude key that opens a door is better than none at all, and when applied to an ostrich or a penguin it seems to me that sense is made of actions that have been otherwise hard to understand. For the ostriches of Africa and South America are peculiar in their breeding habits, although peculiarity perhaps applies to all of us in some degree. Male ostriches are both masculine and maternal, females are just female

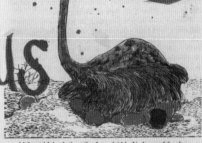

Male ostrich incubating pile of eggs laid by his harem of females.

a matriarch, from season to season. A stag is masculine and paternal ... ... ... female. In red deer, maternal ... last often until the third year of life of the offspring, and it is once again this matter of milk and the solicitude that grows out of it that gives stability to the family and cohesion to the group. The hinds associate and ... may have two or three followers, and even some of their ... hinds may be offspring of a hind still within the group. A mature and older hind leads each group of hinds and ... followers, usually with a calf of her own along-side. She needs to be a breeder, it seems, in order to

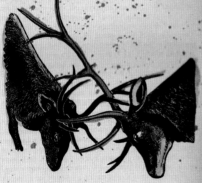

Stags in combat, with clashing antlers.

maintain her leadership. And within such a social group, bound together by milk and maternity for years on end, mutual education and the exercise of intelligence develop as far as the ... of deer permits them. Yet in inter-preting ... as we need to remember that a deer and a man are alike in what the senses mean to them, whatever ... they may be in common between two minds. For the most meaningful sense to a deer is smell; then comes hearing, while sight comes after, for vision is ... blind and eyes are so placed that while the range is panoramic ... the ... ... little ... of deer ... is ... ... perceiving. ... one ... which ... ... in direct movements ... of ... ... ... ... to ... size of life, to ... smell. Sight ... ... to ... can see, but the world ... ... ... flooded with aromas.

Milk production lasts throughout the year and this alone denotes continuing formation of pituitary pro-lactin ... and maternal attitudes accompany the milk. The ... here that means so much is continuity; there is ... when the maternal feeling are allowed to lapse. Soon ... such outcome and feeds upon itself. Milk and hormones flow within the group, no matter how the individual fares, and solicitude goes beyond the immediate blood relationship, as a naturalist in the Sierras discovered. For, while bending over an injured fawn, he looked up to see nine hinds converging on him with anxiety and trepidation mixed together.

There ... order ... with ... group of hinds comparable to a peck ... ... the species, although in unobtrusive ways, with little female ... some bickering ... may go on. The leadership of the dominant hind ... subtle but unquestioned, and so is that of the second ... who acts as her assistant—and it has nothing in common with the

growing from an '79 66 is a HAZARDOUS performance ... and most of us ARE LUCKIER than we realise *

# Rituals for Change

In conversation with Ivor MacAskill, December 2018
Performance text: Battersea Arts Centre, June 2017

> 'The other thing I thought is how much of a group effort I've always felt this show was. It really looks like a solo performance but there's no way I can ever perform this show on my own, because there's so much stuff. There's the tower, and there's the deconstruction of everything – I finish the performance and I'm covered in clay and I have to go to a shower because otherwise everything I touch gets covered in clay. And that is significant – how much support there's always been around my body in the performing of this show.'

The making of *Rituals for Change* began with a trip to Margate to visit a ceramics exhibition there, because I wanted to explore using clay and learning to throw pots as part of the process. I stayed in a hotel beside the sea and got a good deal because it was a Sunday. I documented the trip on a disposable camera from Boots. This trip coincided with my first prescription of oestrogen and I enjoyed the synchronicity of these things – of beginning a new phase of transition at the same time as the beginnings of a new show. I had a terrible cold and didn't want to take the pills when I was separated from my senses and perhaps wouldn't feel the first sensations in my body. I wanted to be open to it all. I bought a pack of Smarties, sorted the blue ones out and ate those instead. I started taking the little blue pills a few days later, in Brighton, again beside the sea. The exhibition was beautiful – a series of porcelain vessels, suspended in vitrine boxes high above the gallery, partly visible and partly hidden from view. The invitation was to view them from the floor in a lying position, which I assumed. As I lay there, intending to get my money's worth and remain until I felt 'something', a basketball began to smash repeatedly against the tall glass windows, reverberating through the silent galleries – an intrusion that we tried emphatically to ignore. It was fascinating, this interruption – the persistence of the outside world shattering the illusion of safety and calm. A perfect illustration of the violence of the world and the fragility of the spaces we create for reflection and calm exploration. I loved it. I was sad when, eventually, security removed the man who was throwing the ball. I wanted the windows to shatter. I was scared. It felt a bit like the end of the world.

The anticipation and excitement I felt about the potential changes my body was going to go through becuase of HRT was what inspired the show. Enough was being said about the political challenges of being trans; I wanted to offer something that was a celebration.

*Rituals* had been commissioned by Forest Fringe for the Edinburgh Festival the following year (the first time in this body of work I'd had a clear deadline) and I had regular meetings with Ira Brand to discuss how the work was forming. I remember how I'd initially had a great desire to make a show that would be clean and simple, with no mess… Alas, perhaps I don't have that in me! Or maybe it is impossible to reflect on the transformation of a body without causing mess – certainly, my own physical transition has proved messy at times.

> **EMMA** Can we start reflecting on what we did together? I'm finding it really interesting remembering that time, and I guess *Rituals* for me came right in the middle of the last six years. So much about the three pieces that came before was really about figuring out my transness and justifying it and articulating it. Lots of dealing with shame and apologising and working out my privilege and my place in things. And I think *Rituals* was a bit of a shift. Rachel [Mars] said the other day that when she saw *Rituals* she felt like, 'Ok, this is where the work begins,' that everything we'd done [before] had been necessary to get out in order to be able to then make something like *Rituals*. And I felt that was quite a fair comment. But what do you remember from it?

**IVOR** I remember you being in the theatre with lots of bits of paper laid out on the stage and I was like – woah! There's loads here. We mostly started off listening to where you were at and listening to the bits of text that you'd written. And this range of ways of thinking and talking about it... The different styles of the text you were writing and the images you were creating and thinking about – some very poetic, some very down to earth, some very medical. So I remember entering that world of you creatively thinking about those things that were happening in your life and how to mark them...

At one point in *Rituals for Change*, I say 'now, now, now' whilst bouncing a basketball on the ground. The entire show could perhaps be distilled to this act, to the impossibility of marking a moment in time. It was a rejection of an ever-increasing public fascination with trans lives that seemed always centred on a moment of transitional change – in search of a single action that marked an unequivocal change from something to something else – as if all of my experiences and the highs and lows of gender dysphoria could possibly be reduced to a single moment. At the time, this assumption was also present in my interactions with family and friends, who were wondering when I might suddenly, seemingly spontaneously, change into someone completely different.

That single moment could be the basketball; the axe chopping the wood; water dripping from a scaffold; even the performance itself, the action of each ritual. In retrospect, the show itself inevitably becomes a time capsule, a frozen moment. But it is impossible for us, as living beings, to remain in suspension; to really choose when things might change. The truth of it is that we are always changing.

**EMMA** It's interesting remembering it all laid out on stage... The film of *Rituals for Change* was showing at the weekend at this fringe festival in Hackney and was put up against another piece called *Ripples*, [that the creators spoke of] as being a collage. It was made around a fashion designer and some of their work, and the different locations were all kind of collaged together. And I thought that was a really perfect piece to put *Rituals* against. 'Cause although *Rituals* feels quite cohesive now, because of its 'dramaturgical tightness' and the fact that we've been performing it for a while, to me it feels like such a collage of different things. And that was certainly part of what we did together. I definitely didn't sit and write something that was sixty minutes through, I wrote tons and tons of paragraphs and snatches and sentences and bits and pieces. Which I guess for something that's trying to articulate lots of different moments and bring them all together was quite appropriate. Definitely felt like a collage.

**IVOR** And I think that reflects the process of a transition, where time feels very strange. You can always definitely say, this time in a year I'll be like that. And you can mark it and then look back. But at the same time it's a big swirling stew of stuff, and it doesn't follow that nice neat narrative. But you're trying to make sense of yourself and people over time. So I think the process of making a piece is very much like the process of making yourself through that transition.

**EMMA** I totally agree, and I think the process of transition is absolutely like that. But then – certainly for us within the UK, being inside that medical system – the process by which you have to articulate your transition or the way it's spoken about outside the trans community is much more linear, and there's much more of an expectation that there's a story, and it's going to go from A to B to C to D. And so we're all trying to take this thing that's completely made up of different feelings and emotions and contradictions and trying to somehow squeeze it into a narrative that makes a satisfying story, and starts with 'I'm not very happy' and ends with 'I'm delighted with my new body.' And I think that's something that I always want to resist in the work, presenting that kind of neatness. Really with *Rituals*, it surprised me how much of a love letter to transition and to the chemicals that allow my body to transition it is. At the point that I started making it I was just so happy and excited by what my body was potentially going to be going through.

*Rituals for Change* also marked the start of my collaboration with theatre designer and artist Myriddin Pharo. Mydd and I had worked together in our early twenties in Cornwall, but never again until *Rituals*. We met in a carpeted function room and outside in the wild landscape of Cornwall. Surrounded by basic materials – ink, salt, milk, water, earth – we began to explore. Working with Mydd allowed me to prioritise visual and emotional connection above words – a direction I had never worked in before. We spent several weeks getting messy and pushing the work to new places.

One of the key discoveries of this period was China clay – it being a substance that naturally occurs in Cornwall and is used for countless purposes. As well as being the clay from which porcelain is made (which was an interesting connection to the exhibition I visited in Margate), it is also used as the body of many pharmaceutical pills. Working with China clay in its pure powder form, we ultimately developed the final ritual of the show.

> **IVOR** The rituals are interesting because part of their genesis came from these *mysterious rites* that you'd been having in Cornwall. You came in with these pictures of the sea, of clay, all these amazing images, and then it was like, 'How do we weave these into the work?' And how do you retain elements of that, that sense that you're in the forest or you're in the sea when actually you're in a black box studio? And how can we have these spiritual themes while being really engaged to the body, while we're trying to rationalise our existence? I remember that idea that an audience member won't know what [the rituals] are for, or what they're doing necessarily, but that you can sense the importance of them, or the journey they are taking you on. Is it something that you're repeating to remember a feeling? Is it a kind of catharsis, so you're trying to let go of something and get something back? Or are you trying to call something up and join everyone together? What's affecting is that each ritual is doing a job, but part of the job is really creating you as a person and giving you space, and a future, and a way through time.

I constructed five rituals that feel more important every time I enact them. I perform them as if the ritual somehow is my transition and will save and protect me from the difficulties I have encountered – the medical shit; the political shit; the shit in the street. The rituals were originally intended to respond to different relationships with my changing body – my skin, tears, beard, breasts, breath. But over time those meanings have given way to deeper ones. I remember the origin of the ink ritual, where I shake violently and a mix of black ink and salt runs down my body. I had a conversation with movement director Rachel Blackman, who told us about a film she'd seen where a dingo is nearly hit by a car and goes to the side of the road and just starts shaking – really shaking itself – and then it stops, looks around and trots away completely recovered. Literally shakes the trauma out of its body. That's something that's always in my mind at that point of the performance – how can I shake the trauma out? My trauma, my community's trauma?

> **EMMA** I was engaging with rituals in my own life and in my own transition as well, and I guess I had those moments that had felt very profound. Coming from a point of not wanting to be appropriative, as a white British person – what is ritual? I wanted to use materials that felt like they were part of my cultural tradition, so what would come out of Cornwall? I was in conversation with some other trans people recently, we were talking about why all of our practices revolve in some way around ritual. And it feeling like this is something that feels very natural to come to. And then you look at the historic role of trans people in communities around the world, and often we are involved in ritual practice somehow. The rational, Western side of my brain gets spun out by that, but the feeling in my body is completely at one with it. So we had the recipe book which was ink and salt and earth, and we had this idea of what those things are used for in witchcraft or in Christianity, but then also wanting to make something new. And what I quite like about *Rituals for Change*, certainly three years on, is that I do feel significant performing the rituals, 'cause they've become personally significant. I've performed them fifty times, so of course there's a significance to them now, just through having done them and embodied them.

Wherever indigenous culture survives in some way, despite corruption by colonialism and outside influences, we still tend to witness a broader understanding of gender identity than the Western binary of male and female. It is widely supposed that in pre-monotheistic cultures, trans people were held in high regard – as evidenced by the high proportion of images depicting gods and goddesses as gender non-conforming or intersex. *This* should inform our understanding of trans history and existence.

In early 2019, I was invited to South Sulawesi in Indonesia to work alongside Bissu shamans. The Bissu have an understanding of five genders, although these do not translate perfectly into the modern Western trans rhetoric. The Bissu shamans themselves represent the fifth gender – the others roughly translating as cis male, cis female, calabai and calalai. Whilst a person of any gender can become Bissu, most are calabai or calalai. Meeting the Bissu felt like a lot of things coming together for me, clear demonstrations of ritual in action as an everyday service – a duty of care – to one's local community; as well as unequivocal evidence, in the ancient traditions and history of the Bissu, that trans people have existed forever.

The rituals we took part in sometimes involved offerings, dance, costume and make-up, and sometimes took place in the middle of the night, inside a home, in response to a storm raging outside. There was always a purpose: a ritual for safe travels, a ritual to honour our ancestors and, on one occasion, a ritual to provide safety for our (queer) community – both in Sulawesi and around the world. ('Our family,' translated Tamara Pertamina, the Indonesian artist accompanying me.)

Trans people were your clerics; your witches; your healers; and, in the long tradition of societally non-conforming people, we were your performers. For many trans artists, the lines between performance and ritual action are still very close, and *Rituals for Change* is exactly that: a collection of ritual actions.

> **EMMA** There's this thing I read online. A trans shaman wrote: 'It doesn't matter if the magic potions we use are prescribed or made by pharmaceutical companies, they're still magic.'

And I think with *Rituals* I really wanted to – because there's so much guilt and there's so much other stuff that comes with it, and it is really political to say, 'Well, if I believe that a woman can be anything she wants to be, why can't I be a woman who has a beard? Why do I not want that? Why do I have this desire to take hormones that will change my body, if I fundamentally support the right for women to live however they want?' And it feels kinda uncomfortable, and then someone like Paul Preciado says, 'Well some people call me a hypocrite for saying all this stuff and then taking testosterone, but what can I say? I am an embodied creature!' And so I think with *Rituals for Change,* having made so many pieces that were really wrestling with the politics and the theory around trans stuff – which is all really true and really important – there's this other thing, especially if you're a transsexual, which is just about, oh my god, the satisfaction I received from my body switching over from being testosterone-predominant to oestrogen-predominant! The kind of glorious changes that have happened and continue to happen, just how celebratory and magic that is, and I don't think *Rituals* is a shiny show, I think there's a lot of grit in it as well, but there was like – wanting to just forget for a moment, or not having to justify for a moment, why this was great – and then to just go – look!

Ritual felt very present in my life at this time, alongside (and perhaps to balance) the hyper-medical situations I was finding myself in: doctor's office, psychologist's office, laser hair removal salon, endocrinologist's office, hospital, gender specialist clinic. I found myself creating and engaging with small rituals, trying to connect to and honour my female ancestors – something that became very important as I began to feel more confident in my identity as a woman, and in the face of rejection from some areas of my living family. I have only found love and acceptance from my parents and siblings, and my mum's presence in *Rituals for Change* is very significant. The ceramic pots were thrown on her wheel, and her voice accompanies the final ritual, a recording of her teaching me how to throw my first pot. The recording is largely indistinct amongst the music (composed by my brother Keir) but snatches of words can be heard: 'The pressure between the outside and the inside.' 'It's not the only way.' 'See how I lift my hand off very carefully.' Phrases that can be understood in relation to a changing body and to offering care. More recently, Mum has taken *Rituals for Change* and used it as a starting place for her own art, relating it not only to our relationship but to her own relationship with her body.

**EMMA** This is also something that's really central to *Rituals*, which is why it resonates with people who are outside the trans community as well: it isn't just trans bodies who have this potential to change. It's all bodies. All human bodies! And nature as well. We all have this potential. Some trans people choose to activate that, but we all have it, and that's really quite something. Being caught in this moment, of all the excitement and potential of transition, whilst also being caught in this historical moment where we're under this intense scrutiny, and there's so much justification and also so much political necessity to put a good face on. And be like, hey it's great, we're all super happy, because if you weren't super happy why would you do it?

**IVOR** I think that is quite difficult to handle while you're dealing with [transition] stuff as well, having to present that brave face, or that not-brave face. 'I don't have to be brave anymore, because the wonders of medical technology mean that I'm all better.' And that you should be able to be an advocate and be representing all of the trans community, or communities, or that there *is* one trans community. All that is not easy when you got a few things going on about yourself.

**EMMA** Absolutely. I don't think I've often felt that I could express all of the vulnerabilities that I feel and have felt since transitioning. Pretty much for me with a medical transition came the necessity to be the person who was really totally sorted and fine with it, and [had] to look after other people's feelings about it. And I don't know how much of that is in

*Rituals.* I think I have used the rehearsal room as a way to get my head around some of the things that I feel about myself.

**IVOR** That's what we were talking about a lot – where are the ways in for people? And what are the ways for you to not feel vulnerable while you're on stage? So lots of what we were doing was – how can you be totally kickass on stage, and what of your body do we show, what do we do so that you have time to be in right zone and the right space and take your time at the beginning of it? And to have control, so it's definitely a performance rather than you simply baring your soul. Working with such personal details and using the performance work as a way to work through ideas and the processes of transitioning, I guess there was concerns or worries about – who can this reach? And some of the work we were doing was definitely to find the universal ways in for people. What are the ways for you to be completely in control of this, so that you're not actually having to be vulnerable on stage? And making really clear decisions about when and how your body is seen on stage, and how you can be the most strong within that piece. So that nobody is worried about you, and it's not about the vulnerability that you have, but we see that vulnerability within it. Using theatre in some ways to abstract what is very personal into something that is performed. Even the idea of performing the rituals, while at the same time them being real rituals for you to do, it gives you space, and it gives an audience space, to be able to not worry about you during the work.

**EMMA** Which I think is really important. I remember discussing about – I really wanted to show off my body. Because I was super proud of it, and here's my changing body, and I remember there being the question of – how much of my body do I show? How much of my body can be naked? How much of my body needs to be naked? And then this moment where I'm topless for a moment, how that has felt, and how that changes given how I perceive the audience and who the audience is.

More than any piece in the series, *Rituals for Change* has resonated with people of all identities, but the best response has been from other trans folk. An artist friend told me that seeing *Rituals* was the first time that she realised she was a trans woman. *Rituals* marked a shift for me and my performance – from asking a cis audience for recognition and acceptance to sharing something of myself. When it was first performed at the Edinburgh Festival in 2016, it definitely felt like a different narrative and tone to other shows that were speaking of trans issues. Even the decision to not have an explanation at the start felt like a radical action.

> **EMMA** I think there has been a real thing of, 'Wow how validating that other people find this narrative familiar!' And of course they do, because – to quote Paul Preciado again – 'We are all embodied creatures.' So any piece of work that reflects on the having of a body and being seen in that body is obviously going to be universal, 'cause that's a universal experience, having a body. But the spaces that it was being presented in, because of the kind of theatre-maker that I am, I was feeling like, 'Well, where are the trans people? And why aren't trans people coming into these spaces?' And it's because of lots of reasons and it highlights that we are a very marginalised community, and there's so many barriers towards just rocking up wherever, as there are for a lot of other marginalised communities. So that Gender Roadshow week was all about going, 'How can we make a space that is accessible in the best kind of way, that people feel they want to come to, that people feel is going to be relevant to them, that'd be worth giving up their time for.'

With funding from the Wellcome Trust, we created the Gender Roadshow – exploring whether we could tour this kind of work within a context that would feel safe and genuine to a trans audience. Abby Butcher and I put together a four-day schedule of talks and workshops from invited trans speakers (Sabah Choudrey, Ivor MacAskill, Luna Morgana, Travis Alabanza). Each night I performed *Rituals for Change*, and afterwards there would be a late-night event – a cabaret, a film screening, a party – with the intention to provide a variety of safe environments for people to access the work. One night, the performance of *Rituals* was billed as trans-only: the audience invitation was only for people who identified as trans or were questioning their identity. It's the only time I've performed this piece to an audience I knew to be trans-identified.

> **IVOR** It was a really amazing performance. And to recognise the power of having those sorts of spaces, and for your work to be seen in that way... It's different for a trans audience.

> **EMMA** And there was this moment where I came out to do the final ritual where usually I would be covered with a blanket, and I just had this thought of – I don't have to do that here. There was something, even in a room full of strangers, something about the fact that everybody there had identified themselves as trans in some respect, meant that I felt my body was really safe and they would be able to see my body for what it is, with its small breasts and broad shoulders and Adam's apple – all of those contradictions – in a really non-shocking way. And there was this beautiful moment where I was able to just think, 'Oh I don't need that blanket today!' And then I performed it and it felt so liberating – it felt really nice to be naked in that context, to be seen in that context.

In 2018, we received funding from the Space to translate *Rituals for Change* into film. We shot it over four days in different locations in Sussex and the result is available to view in full online (see p. 223). It was something we had wanted to do for a very long time – in response to the difficulties in accessibility for a trans audience and recognising how much easier it is for some trans people to access digital content. Whilst there is lots of trans-generated online content, the vast majority seems led by information, rather than art. We did not want to simply film the stage show and present a second-rate experience; instead, we asked what the medium of film could provide that cannot be recreated in a live performance – something that would complement the live experience, rather than compete with it. Mydd and I went back to our original development period, to the outdoor rituals, and we decided to film the four key moments on location, in environments that would be challenging to take an audience to. We then filmed the piece in full inside The Spire, a deconsecrated church that now operates as an arts venue in Brighton. We shot it all in only four days, and over those four days experienced every type of weather imaginable – encountering driving rain on the beach, wind and sunshine in a cement foundry and, most excitingly, snow on the day we shot the clay ritual in some woods.

I am pleased that we recorded the piece at the time we did – following well-received performances in London, São Paulo and Jakarta, and at the peak of its resonance with me. It feels necessary that I outgrow the production, as its core message is one of change, fluidity, and moving on. Film is a way of cheating this natural progression however and holding a moment in stasis, forever – after all, so much has already changed since the inception of *Rituals*.

**EMMA** Are there any moments that you can put your finger on, since making this to now – do you feel that there's a different context, politically, going on for trans lives?

**IVOR** Absolutely. What's interesting for me is that now my social world is more saturated with trans stuff. There's more trans people on my social media feeds, I'm more aware of stuff going on, which means I'm more aware of the backlash that happens against trans visibility. Because I feel like I'm kind of new to it, I want to know everything, but then as soon as you start to let that in it's like – 'I don't want to know that!' I don't want to know that there are people who don't know me who think I shouldn't exist. So there's this, 'Look at all these amazing wonderful people living their lives and doing what they need to do!' And then you have the people who don't want you to do that. And then I'm being told that I have to be even more of an oppressed minority than I was when I was identifying as a lesbian, or being just queer. So that's definitely a change. I wouldn't change it, but it's quite a big change. Even though it's still personal and there's so much individual soul-searching, now you're part of this other big thing that you have to engage with.

**EMMA** It's funny 'cause you say you wouldn't change it, and I was thinking like, 'Oh, I mean, surely we would change it to be like, not bad, if we could?' But I think there is something in the experience that I probably wouldn't change, and whilst of course I would change violence against trans people and bullshit misinformation and all that kind of stuff, what I wouldn't change is my journey from living as a guy (although I never was that, but being accorded all of that privilege) to today – I feel so lucky, I feel so lucky to have been able to have that experience. When I was first doing my illicit research into being trans, and trying to find people on the internet, and reading blogs, and looking on Tumblr and all of that kind of stuff, there were so many radical voices and really politically engaged trans people, that I really was given this sense of, liberation has to be for everyone, it can't just be for the Caitlyn Jenners of this world. And that's something that with the increased visibility I'm not sure I always hear so much in trans discourse.

**IVOR** What shifts am I making within my own existence? And does that connect with other people? I guess I'm excited about the place we're in and the potential of where we're at, but it feels like a hard struggle to go through as well.

**EMMA** It is a very engaging time to be in transition, and particularly engaged with trans issues, and making art around it. And I certainly welcome the energy that is around at the moment. It's tough and it's tougher for a lot of people than it is for us. But I do feel that increasingly we have spaces to check in. That's an optimistic point to end on!

When I wrote *Rituals for Change* I was hopeful, nervous, apologetic of claiming the word 'woman', of daring to share my stories of abuse.

Now I know I am a woman, that I am abused and angry. And I am powerful.

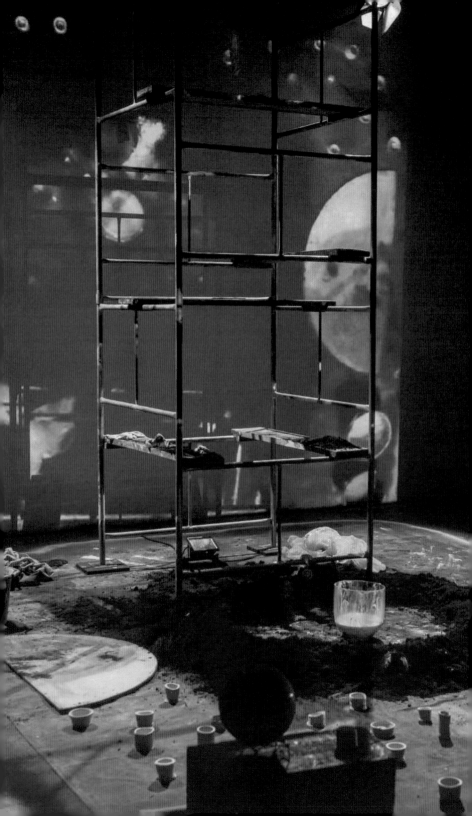

# RITUALS
# FOR
# CHANGE

TO ALLOW OURSELVES TO HEAL IS THE RADICAL ACT

**2015**

**MUSIC**    **Seu Jorge's cover of David Bowie's
'Changes' plays on the record player – it is
in Portuguese, vaguely recognisable.**

*Emma is setting clay pots around the stage.*

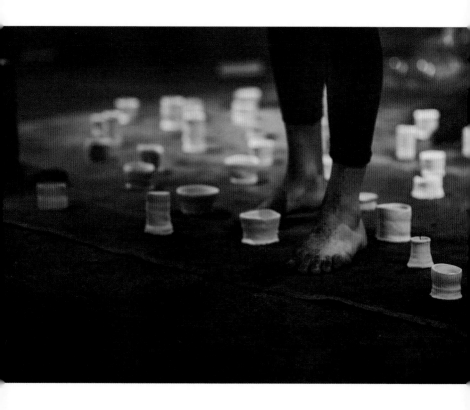

**MUSIC**     **Emma puts the classic blues song 'Mannish Boy' by Muddy Waters on the record player.**

*Emma is chopping wood with an axe.*

**The track ends.**

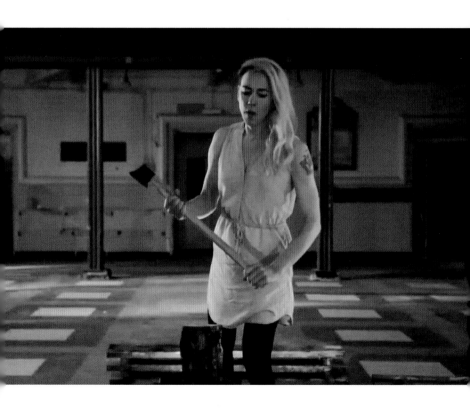

*Emma binds her left hand to the chopping block and raises the axe.*

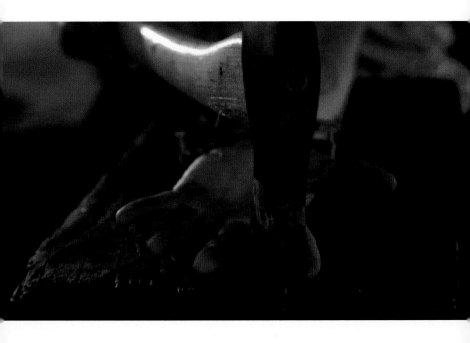

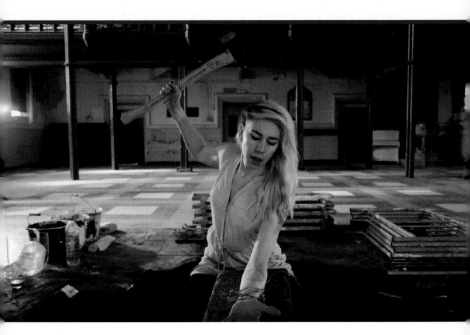

**If I cut this finger off. We can say**

That there was a moment, when I went

From having five fingers to only four.

A before and an after. A moment

Of change. Clear and unequivocal.

But can we not also say her whole life

Had been leading up to this moment and

That the five-fingered future was never

A possibility anyway. That

**There is no A and B, only a flow**

**From then to now to then...
a progression**

**Of change so slow it cannot
be perceived,**

**Like a glass window grown fat
at its base**.

And the person you are today, is that

The same person you saw ten years ago

In the mirror? A close relation or

A total stranger? Do I do this or

Not or does it simply arrive one day,

Unannounced? The change not visible

Until the moment has passed because, really,

How often can we mark that exact moment?

We cannot place our finger on the tide,

But there is an obsession to know when

**The axe will fall.**

**The radical act is to exist.**

**The radical act is to be seen,
to choose to allow others
to see these radical bodies.**

**To allow ourselves to heal
is the radical act.**

*Emma moves the block of wood forward and places a pot on it.*

**There is a card in the tarot
that represents radical change –
it's called The Tower.**

*She illustrates the following text with a pile of earth.*

**There is all-consuming fire;
a vast heaven; a fiery sun
(which is sometimes an eye).
There is a solar eclipse;
there is lightning.
There are two figures in mid-air
either jumping or falling.
One of the figures is on fire.**

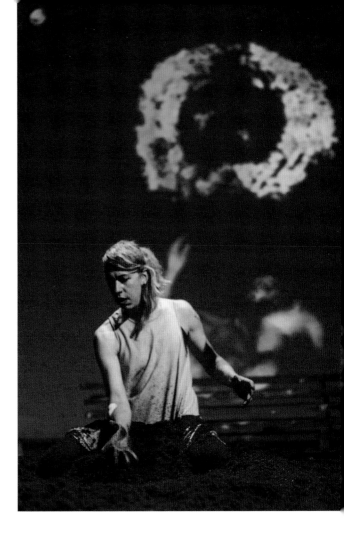

It represents a change so sudden
and fierce that the only options
are to be consumed by the fire,
or to leap and either plummet
to the ground or soar into the air.

**MUSIC**            **An upbeat blues song plays on the record player.**
**It's 'Got my Mojo Working' by Muddy Waters.**

*Emma builds a scaffold tower to the first level.*

*She bounces a basketball. It reverberates through the space.*

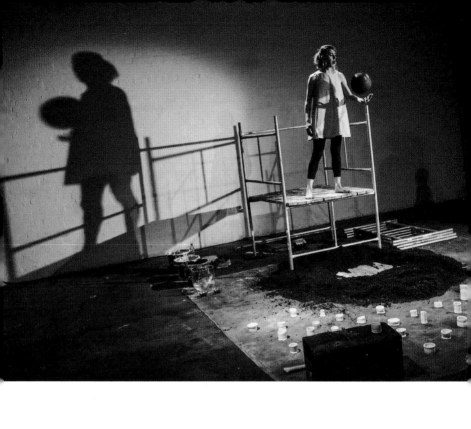

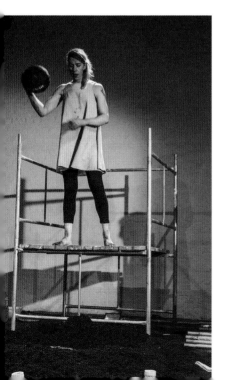

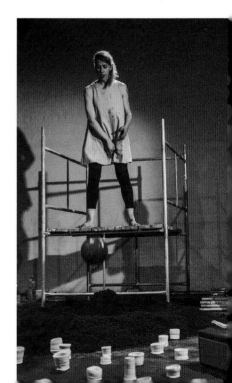

It is tempting to see this as a punctuation –
a moment in time when the ball lands.

**here.**

**here.**

**here.**

Instead of seeing the whole journey from the moment the ball leaves my hand to the moment that it returns.

**Or the journey from Sports Direct to the back of my cupboard.**

**Or the journey from China to the car boot sale.**

**Or the journey from the tree to the scrapheap.**

**From clay to pot.**

**At what point in the process does it stop being one thing and become the other?**

# SALT

RITUAL 1

*Emma marks the edge of the space with salt.*

**MUSIC**  **Ritualistic harmonic music – 'Christopher Fox: Concurrent Air' by Delta Saxophone Quartet.**

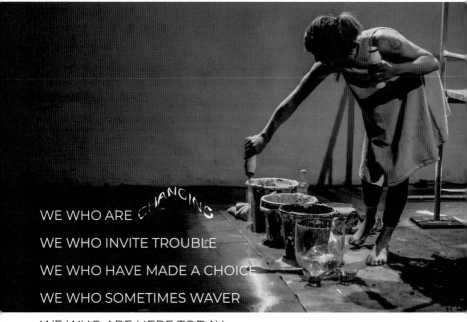

WE WHO ARE CHANGING

WE WHO INVITE TROUBLE

WE WHO HAVE MADE A CHOICE

WE WHO SOMETIMES WAVER

WE WHO ARE HERE TODAY

WE WHO BREATHE

WE WHO ARE MEAT AND WATER
AND BLOOD AND STUFF

WE WHO WATCH

WE WHO LISTEN

WE WHO BREATHE TO A RHYTHM

WE WHO HAVE THOUGHTS AND PLANS
AND DATES AND OTHER PLACES TO BE

WE WHO LEAVE THIS ROOM CHANGED

FROM WHEN WE CAME IN

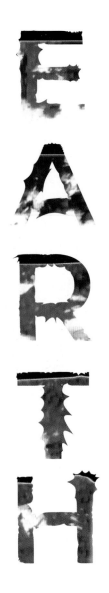

EARTH

RITUAL 2

*Emma digs into the earth beneath the floorboards and removes a black dress.*

**MUSIC**      **Discordant loud music – 'Corps' by Zs.**

**The track fades out.**

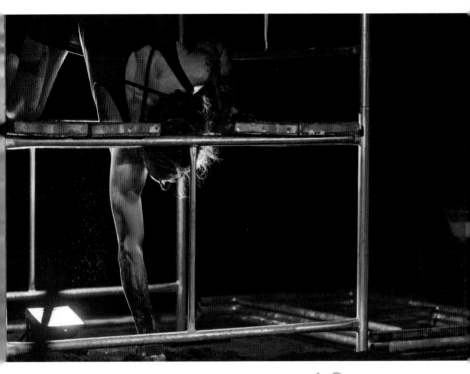

### We are made of water

Bags of water dragging ourselves around – collections of water incased in tight sacks – attractive sacks. Sacks with hair in interesting places – faces that are nice to look at.

We each have an outside with which we are familiar. We spend time with these outsides. We paint them, dress them. Are familiar with our image reflected in glass – the glass of a mirror or the glass of an iPhone screen or the glass of a glass.

We all possess an interior, a full and fascinating interior life that is constantly moving. There are tides inside of us – oceans of change. Seas in constant ebb and flow.

I am familiar with
We are familiar with 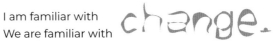 change.

**MUSIC**　　**The sound of the sea plays from the record player.**

*Emma builds the tower higher.*

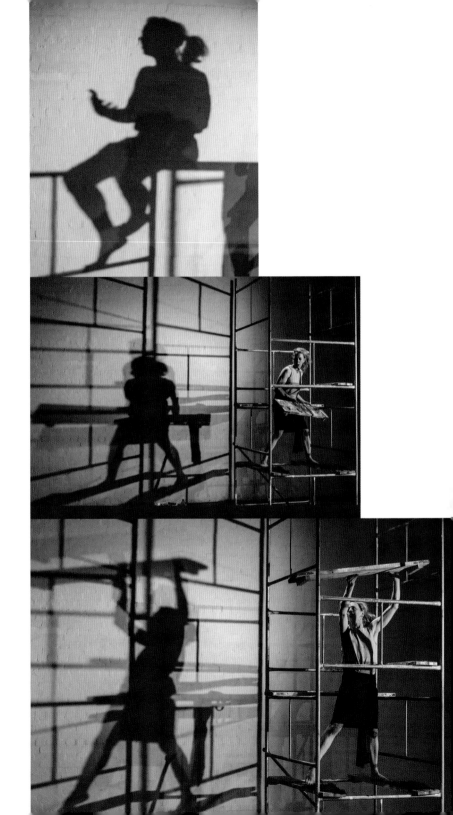

*She carries a clear plastic bag of water to the top and hangs it there.*

*She moves to a ledge and lies down, facing out.*

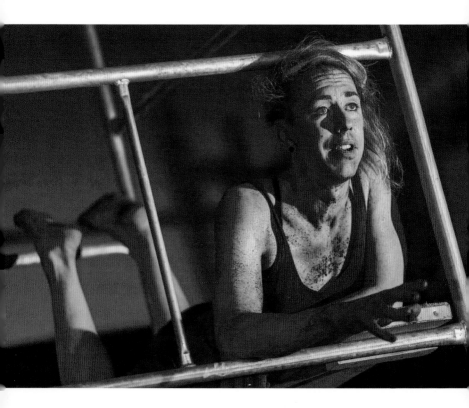

I imagine removing all my clothes and
standing beneath the dripping moss with cool
moving water beneath my feet and I look out
at the perfect blue-green with sparkles and
shimmers and there is a seal in the waves –
held almost motionless amidst the movement
and it takes a breath and I take a breath and
slowly I move into the blue – mixing my flow
with it – mixing this bag of water with all the
water and momentum of the planet and life.

There are no beginnings, but if there has to be
a marker, then this could be a pretty clear one.

It begins in a hotel room in Margate
and it also begins in a doctor's office.
It begins with a nervously entered search term
and it begins 30 years ago in a classroom.

## It begins with a breath.

## It begins with a pill.

I open the blister pack and take out a
small blue pill.
A small blue pill that is made of sugar
and chemicals and clay.

I place the pill in my mouth and then I hold it
beneath my tongue, then I swallow and
I imagine the waves radiating out across
my body – re-writing what they find like
the names left in the sand as the tide rolls by...

I did not know how sick I would become.

This small blue pill that caused
a year of pain, a year of investigation,
a year of being unable to be touched.

A small blue pill became

a silver sachet of gel

a silver sachet of gel
made of chemicals
and petrol and water.

This silver sachet of gel
that made my levels rise
and fall with such alarm
that the doctors could not,
would not know what to do.

So now I wear a patch

a small clear patch
made of plastic
and chemicals and glue.

I place this patch upon my skin
and chemicals enter my body –
they combine with my hopes
and there...they change.

Oestrogen is carried into my bloodstream
and flows around my body until it reaches
different areas and there it changes.

Our bodies are having internal conversations
every day – checking in with themselves –
is this still how you would like me to be?

A complicated system of railroad crossings,
of Morse code, of postcards, of signals between
hormones and receptors.

This is happening within each of us regardless
of if we're actively inviting change. The bag
of water held in flux is constantly seeking
a direction – we constantly ask – is this how
you would like me to be?

**yes,**            **stay like this.**

**yes,**            **stay like this.**

                    **stay like this.**
                    **stay like this.**
                    **stay like this.**
                    **stay like this.**
                    **stay like this.**

**NOW.**      **CHANGE.**

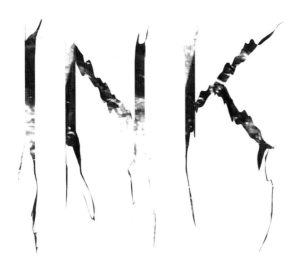

RITUAL 3

*Emma places a mixture of salt and ink inside her bra.*
*She vibrates, softly at first and then with increasing intensity.*
*The ink runs down her body.*

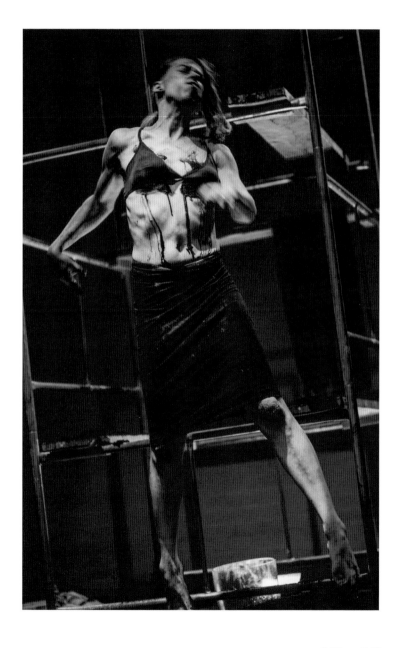

**MUSIC**  **'Brushtones' by Arnold Dreyblatt – single notes from a double bass and an echoing drum.**

**The track fades out.**

Lately I've been getting some funny looks.
More attention from strangers.
Touched by men I have never met.
Approached by people.
Laughed at, tutted at, disapproved of.

I got my first wolf-whistle from some builders
and I think really?
Really?

Looked at in a way that I am not accustomed
to being looked at. Seen as I am not
accustomed to being seen.

And maybe it was because I was wearing a skirt.
Or maybe it was ironic?
A 'fuck you'
rather than a 'fuck? You?'

But either way these new interactions
are not welcome.
The too, too close personal space
and the looking. Really looking.
Looked at.
Not seen.

And I am now complicit in this because
it is the default not an opt-in option.

A body that emits permission to look
or to touch because it is female?
Because it is different? Because it changed?

And I am now complicit in this because
sometimes I feel it validates me.

So I buy into this too.

And I don't want to be the record that is stuck
I don't want to be stuck on this one experience
I don't want to suck the party out of
the room but...

I'm coming straight into womanhood on
the far side of 35 ready for my mother phase,
a parent but not a mother.

And I am scared of getting older – scared of
invisibility, scared if there is no invisibility
because what would that mean?

Because if transition takes 5 years
I'll be 40 by the time I'm there.

With no ramp up and no teenage bedroom
to hide in.

And it seems that every fucking time
I step outside the door something happens.

**I have been** **shouted at.**

**I have been** **threatened.**

**I have been** **scared.**

# REVOLUTION.
# NOW.

# CHANGE.
# NOW.

*She pierces the bag of water.*

YOU WILL BECOME WEAKER

YOU WILL LOSE STRENGTH IN YOUR ARMS

YOU WILL GAIN WEIGHT

YOU WILL BECOME SOFT

YOU WILL WANT TO SLEEP MORE

YOU WILL BECOME IRRITABLE

YOU WILL BECOME INVISIBLE

YOU WILL BE LOOKED AT

YOU WILL BE VULNERABLE

YOU WILL CHANGE

IT WILL BE PAINFUL
BUT IT WILL BE WORTH IT

*Emma drops an opaque roll of plastic –
it covers the tower.*

**MUSIC** **As the roll hits the floor – a series of radio
waves and harmonics with occasional
electric guitar. Eventually a woman's
voice is heard indistinctly – she is
offering advice on throwing a pot.**

**We hear snatches of her words:
'Pressure on the outside and the inside.'**

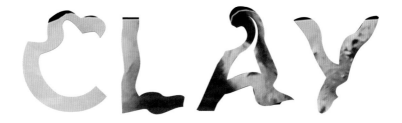

RITUAL 4

*Emma covers her torso and face with China clay.*

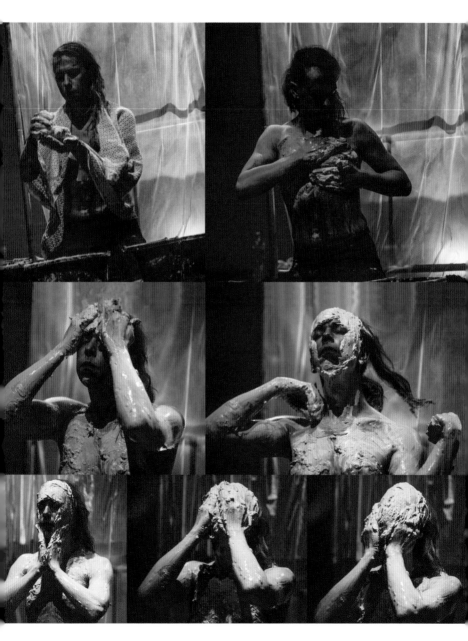

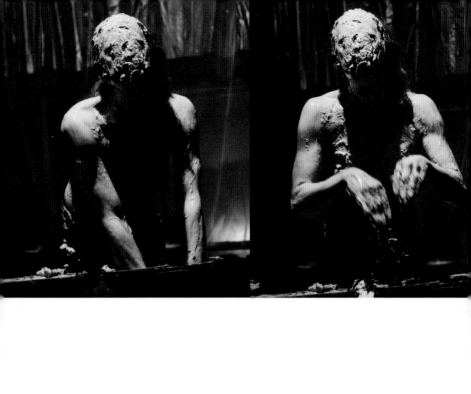
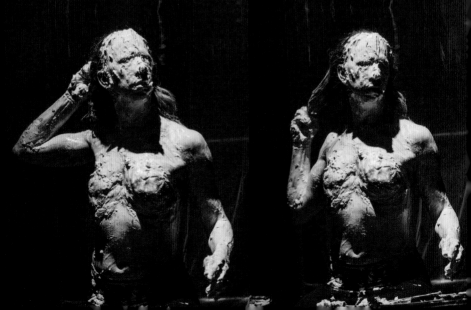

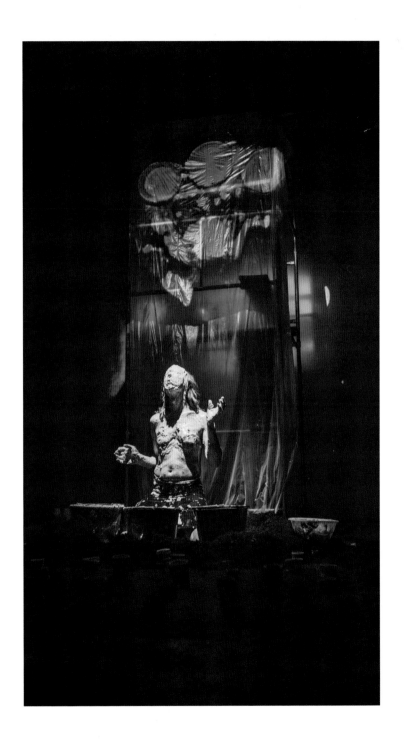

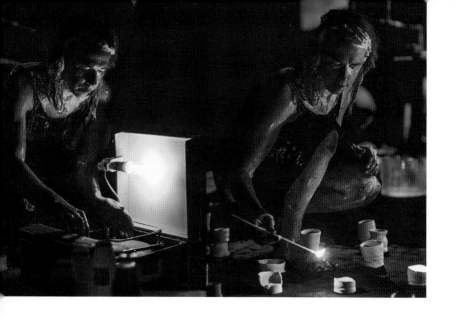

## MUSIC    'Battle Gloves' by Mel Sanson.

*Emma lights candles inside the clay pots.*

*She climbs up to the top of the tower.*

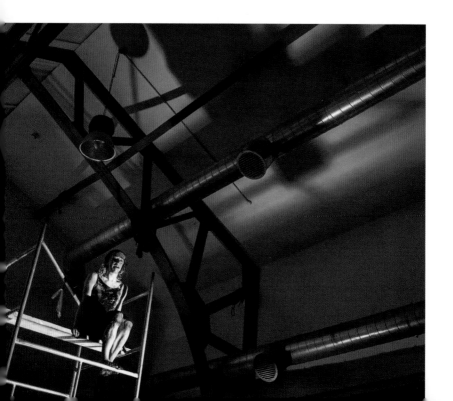

**The radical act**

IS TO EXIST.

**The radical act**

IS TO BE SEEN.

**To choose to allow others
to see these radical bodies.**

**To allow ourselves to heal**

IS THE RADICAL ACT.

WE WHO ARE CHANGING

WE WHO INVITE TROUBLE

WE WHO HAVE MADE A CHOICE

WE WHO SOMETIMES WAVER

WE WHO ARE HERE TODAY

WE WHO BREATHE

WE WHO ARE MEAT AND WATER
AND BLOOD AND STUFF

WE WHO WATCH

WE WHO LISTEN

WE WHO BREATHE TO A RHYTHM

WE WHO HAVE THOUGHTS AND PLANS AND
DATES AND OTHER PLACES TO BE

WE WHO **ARE ENGULFED IN FLAMES**

WE WHO **JUMP**

WE WHO **SOAR**

WE WHO LEAVE THIS ROOM CHANGED
FROM WHEN WE CAME IN

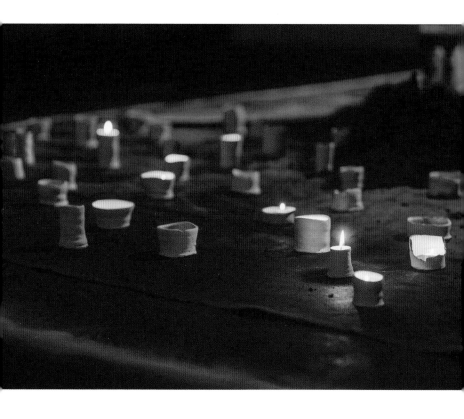

*End.*

**MUSIC**    The original version of David Bowie's
'Changes' plays as audience leave.

# Hearty

In conversation with Myriddin Pharo, March 2019
Performance text: Yard Theatre, February 2018

> 'The ancestors were super close when we made it, weren't they?'

*Hearty* was born of fire. Whereas the previous four shows were attempting to reflect on my experience of transition, or to celebrate the trans body, *Hearty* came about in an increasingly hostile environment and with a growing awareness of a broader global trans experience. I was feeling angry and powerful. I was exploring the science and politics behind the technology we use to bio-hack our bodies and make ourselves. *Hormone Replacement Therapy. HRT. HeaRTy. Hearty. Rituals for Change* had been a celebration of it; in *Hearty*, I wanted to look deeper at the history it was built on – or more specifically, who it was built on top of. I needed to bring fire.

> **MYDD** Because of the whole political thing that was going on at the same time and the anger and the power that you felt, fire was very present in the creation of the show – as a positive, not as a destructive element. Also I think exploring the story and the character and their links to the ancestral female, and the 'hearty sisterhood', brought up a feeling of almost going prehistoric – fire and instinct.

I was fascinated by the fact that *Rituals* had resonated significantly with older menopausal cis women – the same demographic of second-wave feminists who were loudly attacking trans women and positioning themselves as 'trans-exclusionary'. It felt like our shared use of the same bio-technologies (oestrogen pills or patches or gel) formed a strange connection between us. I'd first envisioned *Hearty* as a bridge towards mutual healing and understanding. And then…

A UK theatre programmed Germaine Greer, a widely known trans-exclusionary speaker, as part of their 2017 International

Women's Day events. Although they refused to cancel the event after protests from the local trans community, I was invited to take the main performance space for forty-five minutes and respond to Greer's views. I should note that when it comes to trans-exclusionary arguments, I am of the firm opinion that there is *no debate* to be had: we should not be debating whether or not trans women exist. We clearly do. We have existed throughout history. So – taking the position of #NotADebate, I used my forty-five minutes to sit in silence in front of a banner that read: 'TRANS WOMEN EXIST, THIS IS NOT A DEBATE.' I was joined onstage by Kai Harrison Moore, a BSL interpreter who rested their hands in their lap throughout – an action that made the silence even more palpable. I wanted the image of my body – the presence and reality of a trans woman, existing – to occupy the space for a long period of time; to render ridiculous any argument leveraged against us by a transphobic speaker sharing that same platform.

These events coincided with the early development of *Hearty*, and that's when my desire for it to be a healing project dissipated.

Inspired by the work of American artist Margaret Kilgallen, I began painting phrases and slogans on boards as large as I could find. One of these was in response to a statement made by Greer on the Victoria Live TV show: 'Just because you lop your dick off and then wear a dress doesn't make you a fucking woman.' Late one night, I painted 'LOP YOUR DICK OFF' in large black and red letters on an old piece of board. As with *Language*, I felt that the system was trying to define me by my anatomy, and I wanted to reclaim the statement as a position of power and positivity. I wanted to say, 'Yes! LOP YOUR DICK OFF!' And let the 'dick' be both metaphor and reality; let us take 'dick' to mean privilege and white supremacist patriarchal power, and let's all lop *that* off and dispose of it, in an act of civil disobedience that will change everything. This eventually became the slogan for the T-shirt I wore on stage during *Hearty*.

> **MYDD** I was wondering if that was just my perverted, brutal side thinking, 'That's amazing and in-your-face – we should print it on T-shirts.' But I think conversations we've had together over the years, personal conversations about people's obsession

with what point of transition you are at, and 'have you had it cut off yet' – and what does that even fucking matter?! I think ownership of that statement was exciting, and to wear it on the front of your body as a statement of 'let's get over this question now and let's talk about what is actually important' felt like a good place to start off from. And because it's interlaced with Germaine Greer I think it was reclaiming the power and reclaiming statements. Over the years we've reclaimed words, like 'queer', which is now a really positive thing, and I think it was good for us to reclaim that statement which was once born out of hate and use it as a positive.

**EMMA** And it's funny.

**MYDD** It's funny as fuck. It's all the things that people want to say but they never really say it, and I think in terms of your character on stage it instantly sets up what to expect from you because it's not apologetic in any way.

We sold the T-shirts after the performances, and trans women got them free. Each person who bought one had a deeply personal motivation for doing so, and it reminded me of the universality I discovered in *Rituals*. We can all connect because of our experience of having a body; we may or may not be in possession of a literal penis, but we have all lived in a world that worships them.

Dramaturgically, I was interested in the concept of a cycle informing the structure of the production. The emergence of my own cycle had been welcome and significant, if confusing. After four years on oestrogen and anti-androgens, I could now feel the ebb and flow of my hormone cycle instead of the even flow I used to produce – especially in the week before an injection.

What became apparent after some research was that trans and queer people have experienced throughout history a cycle of violence, acceptance, and massacre. It's not hysterical to feel we must be prepared. It is foolish to suppose that we know better or are more protected than the Two-Spirit indigenous people of Turtle Island in the 1600s, or the queer and gender non-conforming people of Spain in the 1930s, or the Bissu in Indonesia in the 1960s (and again in the 1980s). Or many communities across the world today.

Conversations I've had with people outside the UK show just how tangible that violence is. When I led a discussion with trans and queer people in Brazil last year, they described a 'genocide' of trans people, particularly against the travesti section of the community. ('Travesti' is a term for a trans identity that is used in South America – a reclaimed slur most often used by female-identified people who were assigned male at birth and who often are, or have been, sex workers.) 'We must bury our knowledge until the apocalypse passes,' said one person. I wrote *Hearty* in response to this idea. Where is the apocalypse? In the past or on the horizon? Are we the generation who must bury our knowledge or are we the ones who must dig it up?

The week I started working on *Hearty* I also joined my local roller derby league – the Brighton Rockers. In an introductory email exchange, one of the skaters wrote: 'We are a hearty sisterhood.' This was another slogan that resonated with me, offered me a sense of belonging. I painted it in letters six foot high and made it the back wall of the set, at one point in the show creating a literal shelter out of it. The global community of trans women is a hearty sisterhood; the queer, cis and trans women I skate with are a hearty sisterhood. My strength is bound up in my community. The connection I feel with trans women and femmes is a power – *the* power. As Travis Alabanza has said: we are the gift.

I also wanted *Hearty* to explore the idea of hormones as prosthetics, and how some trans people modify our bodies in radical, beautiful ways. I wanted to have wings and Mydd came up with the idea that they be made out of knives – something that would be powerful and scary. Wearing them feels empowering, tough. They say: 'Don't touch.' As a counter to the artificial wings, I also wore a long rat's tail. I wanted a body part that looked cumbersome and unnatural, a weight to be carried around. It's unclear if the tail is a prosthetic or part of the body I was born with – but at times it is also sexy and unsettling.

**MYDD** It was very clear that you were trying to create a superhero-like mythic personality on the stage that was superhuman, and there's so many different avenues that you could go down in terms of wings and them being feathery or bat-like or whatever, but because we were addressing really aggressive issues it felt to me like – wings are a symbol of power and escapism and strength and it was just following through that pattern of owning that kind of slogan and it all being embodied in one character, so it was like – wings are there for flight, but they are also there to aid the lopping off of dicks or the stabbing of people. And they are often seen as a thing of beauty and strength, and I thought it was important for us to explore them as a thing of danger as well, and about the longing to be accepted, and intimate and sexy, and I thought it was interesting to put something in the way of that. And you then really learnt how to use them in the show down to the opening of the Coke can. They were no longer props or pieces of costume, you owned them. And you had to, 'cause they kept fucking breaking every night.

**EMMA** And that was helpful in proving we were correct in how we wanted them to be. The show didn't work until they worked. Not that I put the blame of the show working or not on the wings – but there was something that didn't quite fly until they were powerful. Because when they were breaking and flapping about they looked weak or like some deformity. And actually it's a weirder metaphor in a trans performance to have a powerful and dangerous prosthetic rather than, 'Oh, I'm a half-formed thing, I'm trying to find my way...' And the tail, I love how gross the tail was – so grim.

**MYDD** That was a joint decision. We talked about what kind of tail it would be and very quickly got to a place where it wasn't a pretty thing. I think we talked about rats' tails, didn't we? It almost found itself – and it does lots of things, it says 'reptile' and 'rat's tail' – when I was making it I put layers of skin on it and then rubbed them off like it was peeling, like how snakes shed their skin. Like it was a rebirth and eventually it was gonna be something different. And each night you dragged it around the space it would get dirtier and dirtier and I really enjoyed that it wasn't pristine. It was something that degraded or ripped – which is what would happen if you had a giant tail.

**EMMA** And I found strength in it as well. I learnt how to whip it around, using the momentum of it, and I could flip stuff over with it, so even though the wings were arguably the thing with power, the tail had power to it as well... And threat.

The wings asserted themselves during our run at the Yard. After some trouble-free rehearsals, the welding broke as I ran onstage on the first night. The wings began to flap freely, shifting my weight as they moved around, making my movements awkward. The next night the knives cut my back to ribbons. I was forced to take the wings off, but I was worried the audience might now read them as something broken or vulnerable – as opposed to them being my choice; fierce and scary. The wings were fixed for the final two nights, and finally the show fell into place. I didn't want our prosthetic choices to be seen as an abomination or a secondary beauty; I wanted to show my gender-hacking as a beautiful decision.

**MYDD** Everything there was really real. Nothing was fake in any way. Like the knives – the knives cut you every night and were digging into your back. The tail was heavy. We didn't make the set out of polystyrene – they were big hefty boards, you could see your struggle and that added to it. We decided very early on that whatever we did had to be real, there couldn't be any lying in it, otherwise you would kind of be lying about what you were talking about. And that's one thing we managed to achieve through light or projection or you lugging boards around. You could feel the integrity – it's dangerous. Nothing is throwaway.

At some point during the making of *Hearty* I began online dating for the first time. I felt sexy and desired – and desirable; something the world attempts to deny us as trans women.

I wanted to unabashedly celebrate and capture that sexiness in *Hearty*, while situating it in the piss and pressure of the apocalypse that is our late-capitalist nightmare.

> **EMMA** I think we moved forwards and then we moved backwards. Or, we moved forwards and then we moved forwards again but the second move forwards has not taken us to a place that's better. And I think we should acknowledge the positives, but I think what is also growing alongside that is bigger and bigger opposition and that is what's scary to me. And it's just not stopping. I hope it will. But at the moment it's getting worse. The unfounded things in the media are beginning to take root in law. And that's what scares me. Our government is currently considering setting up trans prison wings – a special isolation place for trans inmates. And stuff like that is where my caution comes, because they're only doing that because they are worried about how it's playing out in the press and because of this press myth of trans women as abusers, and if you put a trans woman into a female space they're gonna abuse people. And what's a female space that they control? It's the industrial prison system. So they can do something about that in a way that they would like to do in other areas.

We're currently in a time where the media fetishise trans visibility at all costs. I've received invitations to talk and debate on various platforms, and the response I've developed – to ask for remuneration for my time – tends to end most conversations. One such invite was from a company that would only refer to themselves as a 'Global Super Brand' and claimed to be looking for trans people to participate in a 'gender revolution'. I took particular umbridge at the way they were attempting to situate themselves as allies to the trans community, using language of revolution and counterculture to sell their product. They wouldn't reveal their name until I gave my personal information – address, details, preferences. It began to feel scary. Why would I place myself on a list of trans people? Who was controlling the list? My thoughts were with friends in parts of the world where such lists may facilitate the murder and harassment of LGBTQ people.

In Uganda, where gay men were listed in a national newspaper; in Indonesia, where same-sex couples were evicted from their homes; in the UK, where trans activists have been doxxed and have had personal information leaked.

I terminated my discussion with the Global Super Brand and six months later I discovered who it had been... It was fucking ice cream.

In *Hearty,* the Global Super Brand became the spectre of a dystopian government. A threatening presence ready to round up and eradicate trans people once again. *It happened before. It is happening now. It will happen again.*

The show ended on a song. I knew I wanted it to and had been working with Cornish composer Vicky Abbott from the start, who would take my writing or improvised singing and turn it into something incredible. I had wanted a song to share on my first visit to Indonesia; a song that I could sing as an offering. Beginning tentatively and growing in power, the song in *Hearty* speaks of shame and disgust and fear and about not running from those feelings, as I maybe first did – but owning them, embracing them, reframing them as a sign that if something feels shameful then it is probably worth doing. On my second trip to Indonesia, where I met trans shamans in South Sulawesi, I got to share the song, bringing it to one of their rituals as a gift.

At the end of the play, I set the box on fire and sing. I do not see the song as the thing that is inside the box – but the song is a gift. To my ancestors, to my hearty sisterhood, and to myself.

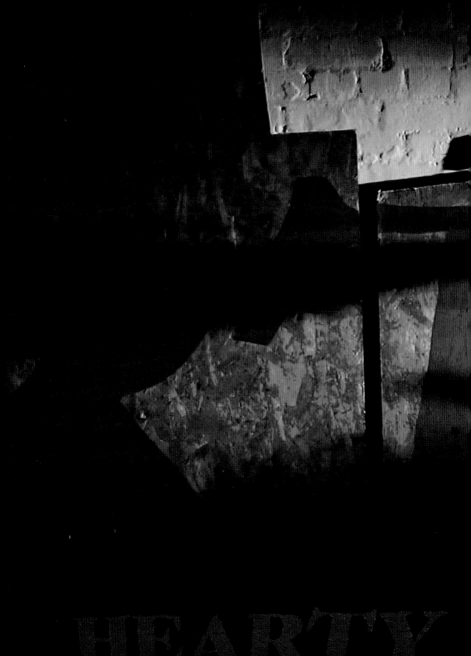

HEARTY

**BURY YOUR KNOWLEDGE
UNTIL THE APOCALYPSE PASSES**

2017

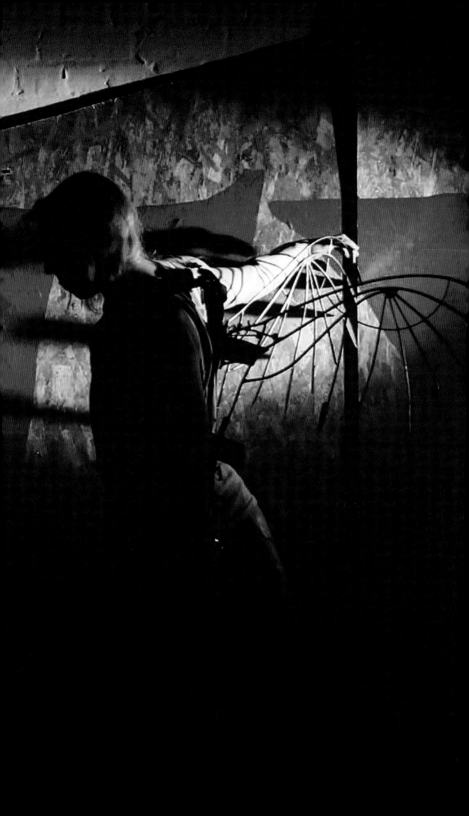

*The stage is glistening and wet.*

*There are boards that read
'WE ARE A HEARTY SISTERHOOD'.*

*A radio device sits off-centre.*

*Storm music plays.*

*We are in the apocalypse.*

# CYCLE 1
# BEGINS

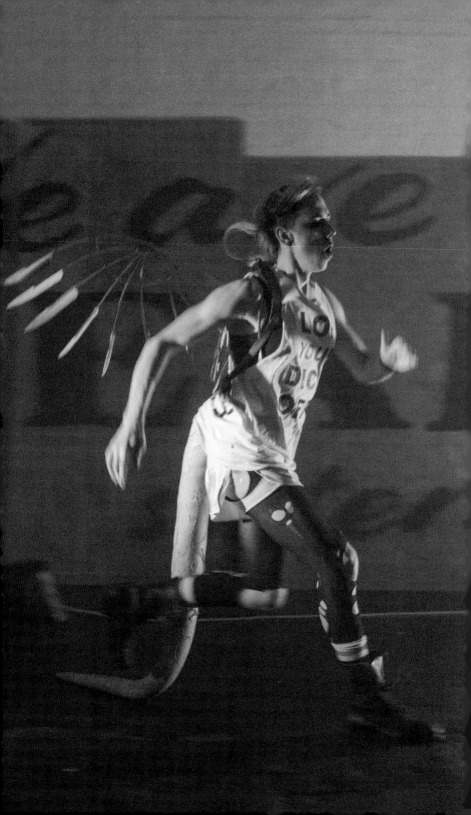

*Music changes
to sirens and noise.*

*She enters running with a large box.*

*She is dressed in a T-shirt that reads 'LOP YOUR DICK OFF'
and she has a tail. She wears metal wings made of knives.
She moves about the space – wings scratching on concrete...
Sharpening, nesting, making safe.*

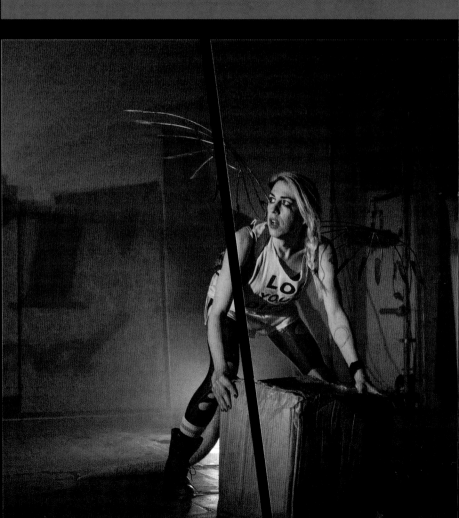

*She picks up a shovel, investigating the box.*

She stands by the box, breathing heavily.

She walks along the boards at the back of the stage, wings scraping along them.

She greedily drinks from a bottle of horse piss.

She shouts some words and begins a furious roller derby warm-up.

We've been here before. We've been here before. We've been here before. Did you hear me?

We've been here before. Been in this place.

Lists are being compiled, attitudes shifting. A place where violence is no longer for fun,

but fuelled by fear.

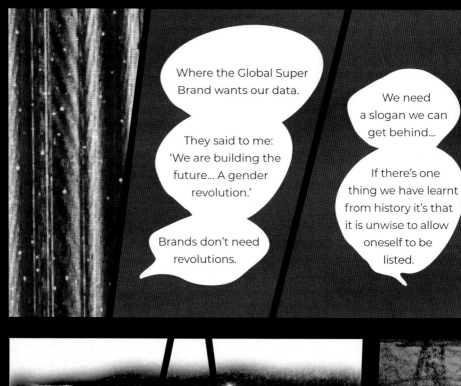

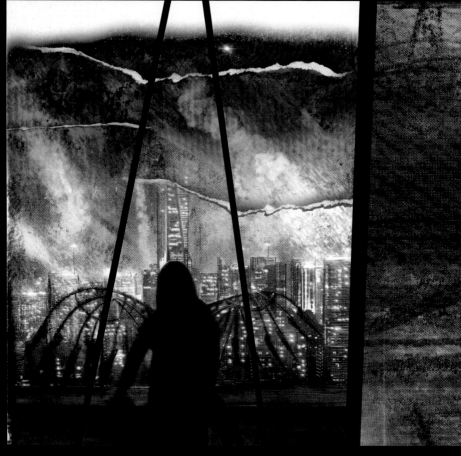

I am in Brazil.

'Está acontecendo um genocídio,' she told me.

There is a genocide.

'Podemos não sobreviver à isso.'

'We may not survive it.'

And so, we must bury our knowledge until the apocalypse passes – bury it deep so that in the future it can be recovered by our people.

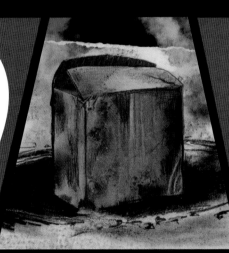

*She looks at the box – and then the mood breaks. She speaks in a different tone...*

And I'm thinking – what the fuck?! What is this future? Where she takes a shovel, stands unafraid and digs?

She digs deep, the sweat beginning to prickle, the earth sticking to her forehead and her shirt sticking to her body, until at last her shovel strikes something. She lifts the casket out – it is old. It smells musty – animal.

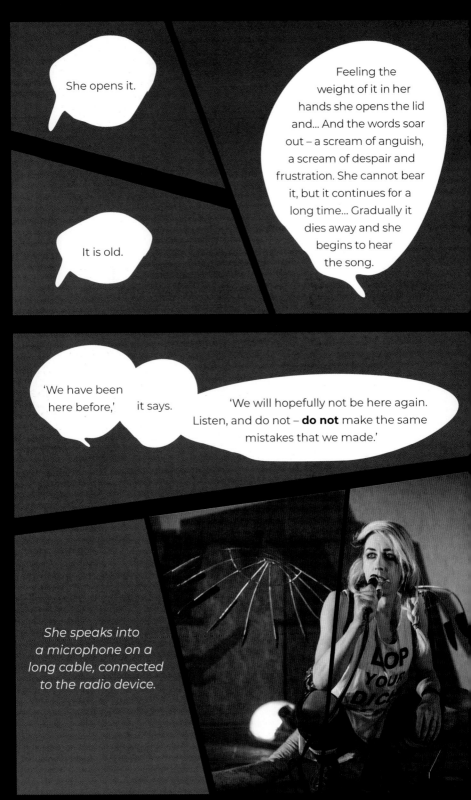

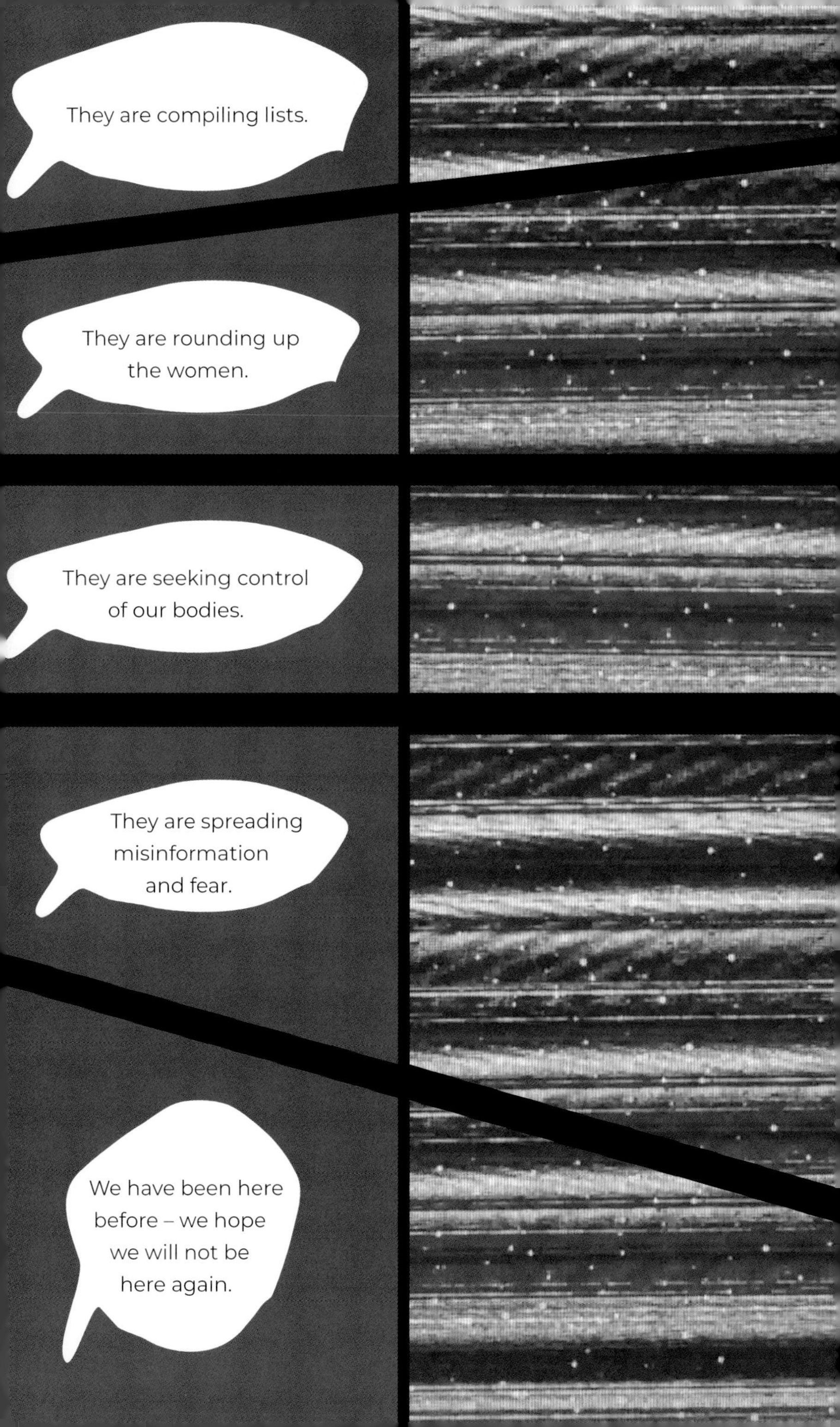
They are compiling lists.
They are rounding up the women.
They are seeking control of our bodies.
They are spreading misinformation and fear.
We have been here before – we hope we will not be here again.

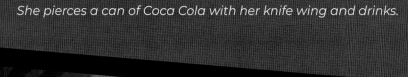

*She pierces a can of Coca Cola with her knife wing and drinks.*

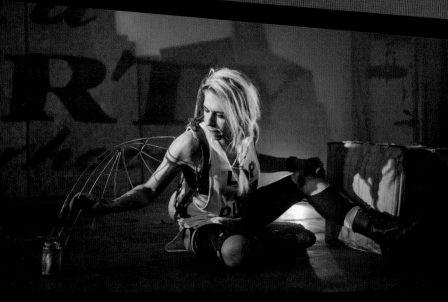

She chooses to wear a device upon her skin. A transmitter, sending bio-codes to her body. It's an extension, a means of connecting with something that is already there.

An add-on, an upgrade, a prosthetic.

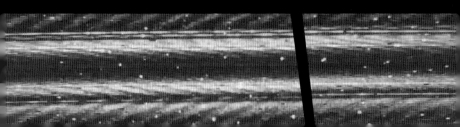

A prosthetic that, when worn,

allows the user to access all kinds of magic.

But all the time,

it is sending data back to the mainframe – where they are watching, listening… Waiting.

The worst thing that ever happened was that people became frightened of witches.

The last thing we need is respectability.

Some sort of noise or theme music. Change of energy – shift.

Stay. Frightened.

Get. Ready.

She is sharpening her wings with a tool.

Slogans are projected on the wall:

BURY YOUR KNOWLEDGE

SHE WOULD SOMETIMES THINK

HE CALLS ME DADDY

WE HUMANS HAVE BEEN DOING THIS

TAKE HER AWAY

WE HAVE NO HISTORY

WHICH CHANGES

THEIR EXISTENCE IS VALID

I LIVE IN A WORLD WHERE PLENTY
OF THINGS I THOUGHT IMPOSSIBLE

I LIKE WELL

UNTIL THE APOCALYPSE PASSES

SHE HAS LOST THE BATTLE

THAT IS MY REBELLION

SINCE BEFORE WE WERE HUMANS

SO HER MUM WON'T SEE

BECAUSE IT WAS ERASED

EVERYTHING

AND ACKNOWLEDGED

ARE POSSIBLE

AND ALLOW IT

So I'm in bed with this girl. Being seduced by her I guess, and she says :

'I've never been with someone who has wings before – how do you have sex?'

And I'm like,

'Thanks for asking... Let's find out.'

My body exists in multiple dimensions at the same time. The one lying in bed with you now and the one in my mind.

One in the future and the one from the past.

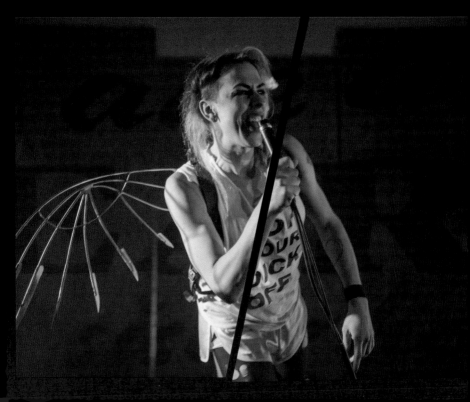

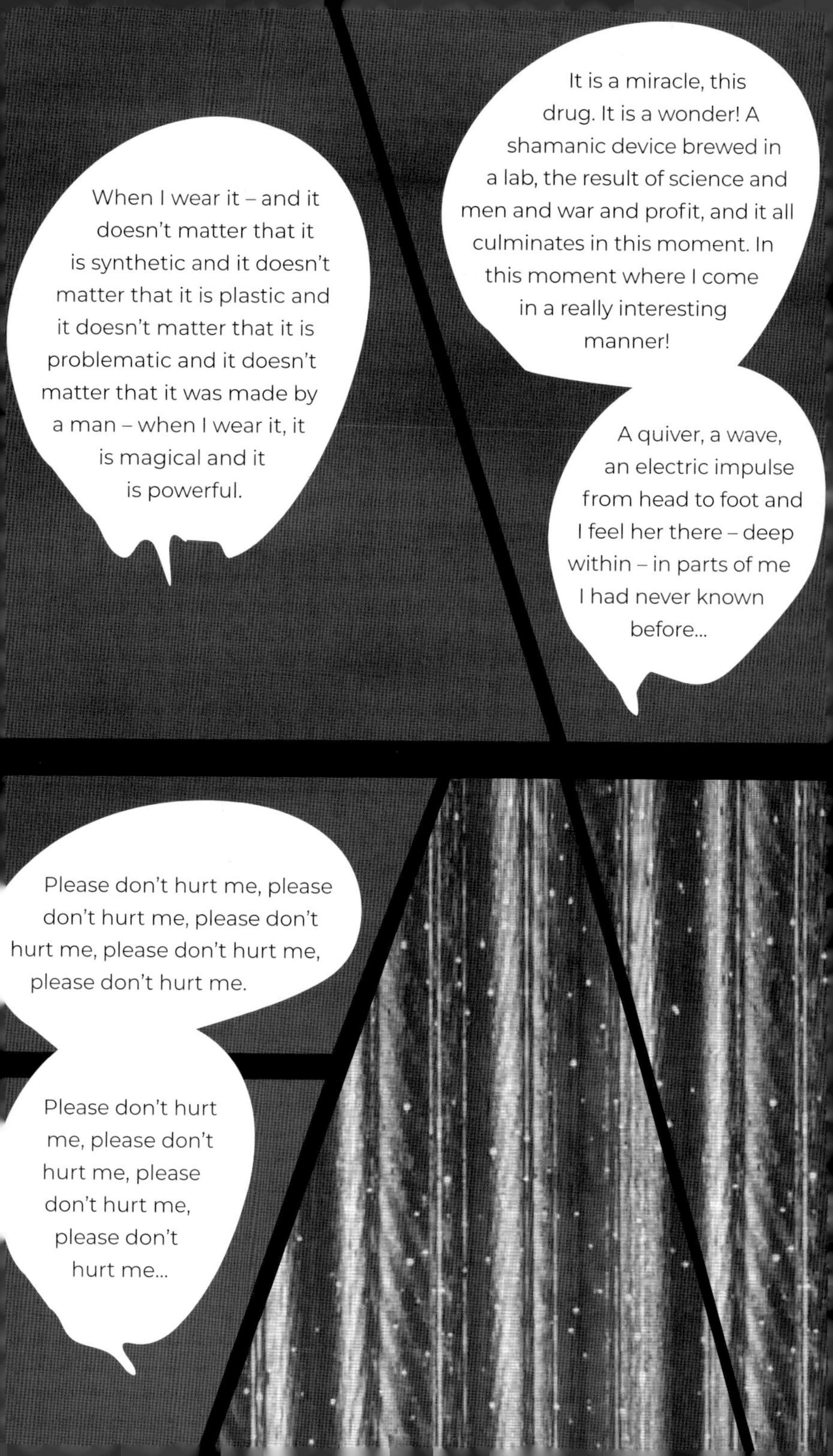
When I wear it – and it doesn't matter that it is synthetic and it doesn't matter that it is plastic and it doesn't matter that it is problematic and it doesn't matter that it was made by a man – when I wear it, it is magical and it is powerful.
It is a miracle, this drug. It is a wonder! A shamanic device brewed in a lab, the result of science and men and war and profit, and it all culminates in this moment. In this moment where I come in a really interesting manner!
A quiver, a wave, an electric impulse from head to foot and I feel her there – deep within – in parts of me I had never known before...
Please don't hurt me, please don't hurt me, please don't hurt me, please don't hurt me, please don't hurt me.
Please don't hurt me, please don't hurt me, please don't hurt me, please don't hurt me...

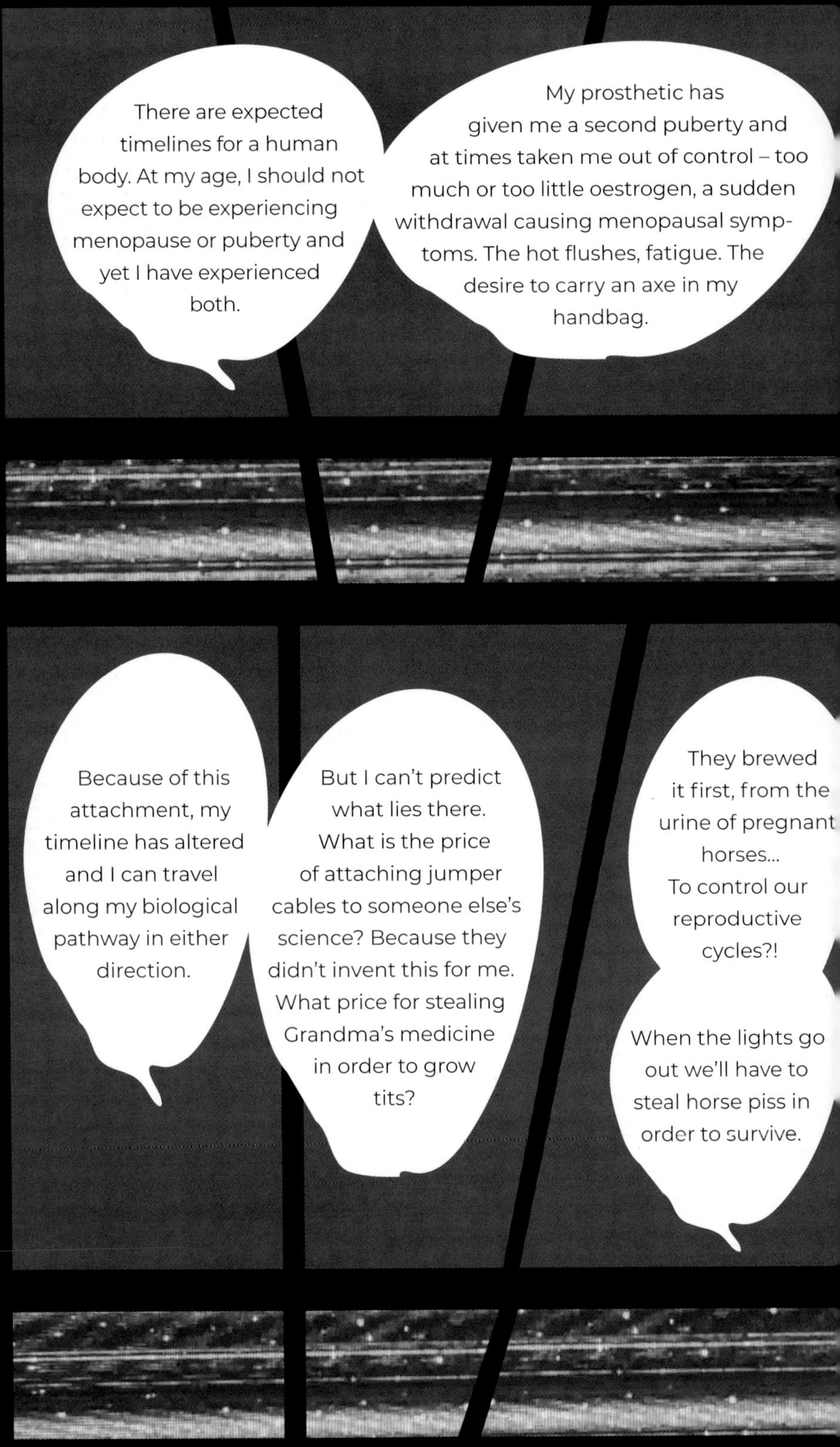
There are expected timelines for a human body. At my age, I should not expect to be experiencing menopause or puberty and yet I have experienced both.
My prosthetic has given me a second puberty and at times taken me out of control – too much or too little oestrogen, a sudden withdrawal causing menopausal symptoms. The hot flushes, fatigue. The desire to carry an axe in my handbag.
Because of this attachment, my timeline has altered and I can travel along my biological pathway in either direction.
But I can't predict what lies there. What is the price of attaching jumper cables to someone else's science? Because they didn't invent this for me. What price for stealing Grandma's medicine in order to grow tits?
They brewed it first, from the urine of pregnant horses... To control our reproductive cycles?!
When the lights go out we'll have to steal horse piss in order to survive.

What do I want?
What do I want?!

What am I?
What should I ask of nature?

A plastic patch for travelling in time, extra arms for embracing, a heart that beats a samba rhythm, pills that make me live longer,

an implanted processor that provides immunity to cancer, a mental download for emotional robustness, a telescopic cock that is easily washable, synthetic tears that come in a bottle.

I want a longer tail so I can tickle you, I want a tongue so long that I can taste you from the other side of the room...

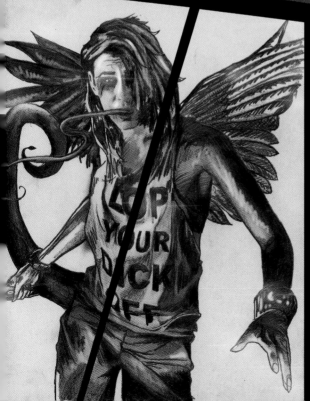

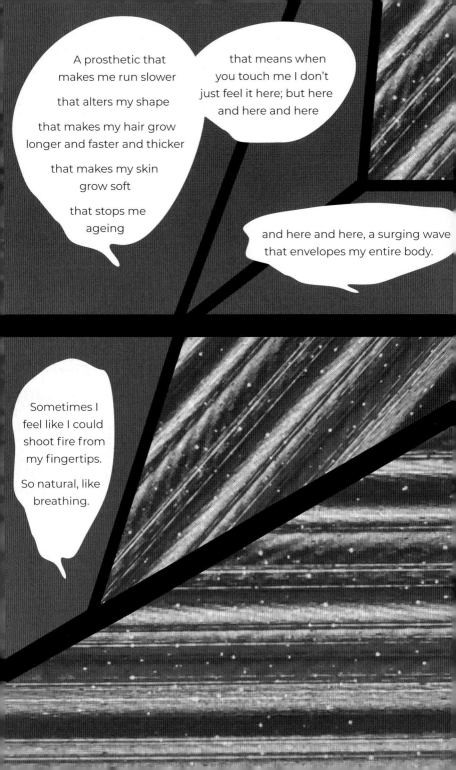

*When we return she has moved one of the boards and is throwing knives at it. Some bounce out. Eventually one sticks.*

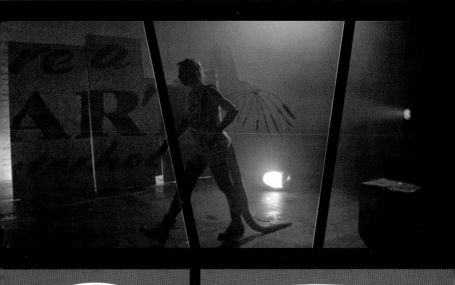

Every cause
is invisible.

Every form changes.

Every timespan
works itself out.

I am consumed by ungovernable desires,
I drink in the seductiveness of a fantastical
world, I stand aghast at its voluptuous error. I
move between ages – standing on the cusp
of a power that can be unlocked.

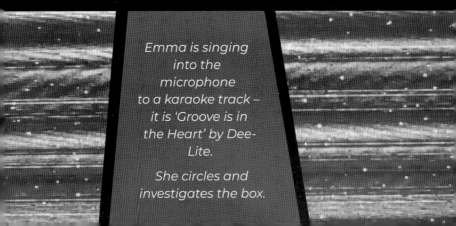

*Emma is singing
into the
microphone
to a karaoke track –
it is 'Groove is in
the Heart' by Dee-
Lite.*

*She circles and
investigates the box.*

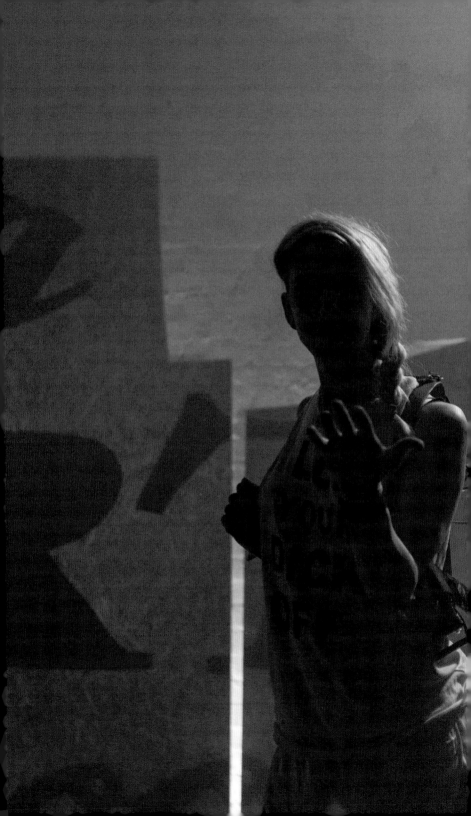

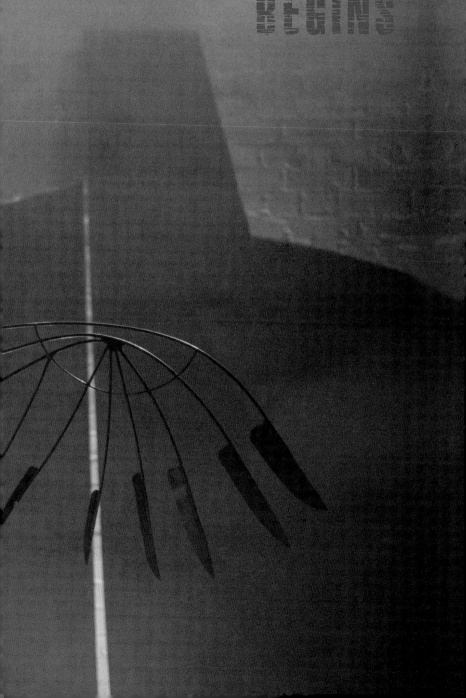

CYCLE 2
BEGINS

She stands with the box, listening for any sound.

She walks along the boards at the back of the stage, her wings scraping along them – one of the boards is missing.

She desperately drinks horse piss.

She shouts some words and begins a furious roller derby warm-up.

We've been here before. We've been here before. Did you hear me?

We've been here before. Been in this place.

Lists are being compiled, attitudes shifting. A place where violence is no longer for fun,

but fuelled by fear.

Where the Global Super Brand doesn't believe we exist.

Brands don't lead revolutions.

We have always been here.

They said: 'Lopping your dick off doesn't change what you are.'

It doesn't change what I am, it changes EVERYTHING else. Whether we do it or not. The potential changes everything.

*She indicates the slogan on her shirt.*

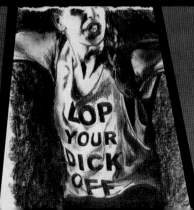

We need something we can all get behind.

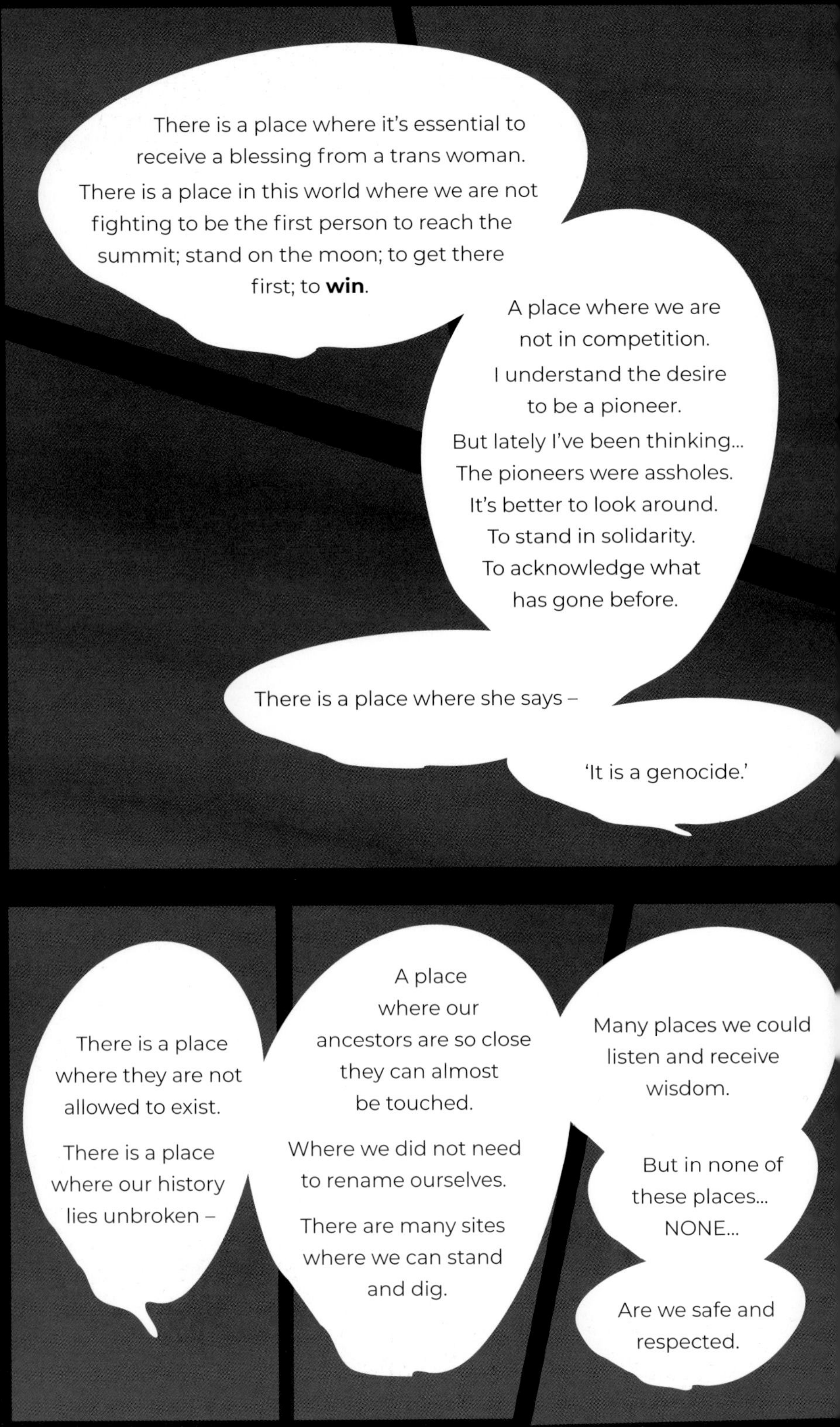
There is a place where it's essential to receive a blessing from a trans woman. There is a place in this world where we are not fighting to be the first person to reach the summit; stand on the moon; to get there first; to **win**.
A place where we are not in competition. I understand the desire to be a pioneer. But lately I've been thinking... The pioneers were assholes. It's better to look around. To stand in solidarity. To acknowledge what has gone before.
There is a place where she says –
'It is a genocide.'
There is a place where they are not allowed to exist. There is a place where our history lies unbroken –
A place where our ancestors are so close they can almost be touched. Where we did not need to rename ourselves. There are many sites where we can stand and dig.
Many places we could listen and receive wisdom.
But in none of these places... NONE...
Are we safe and respected.

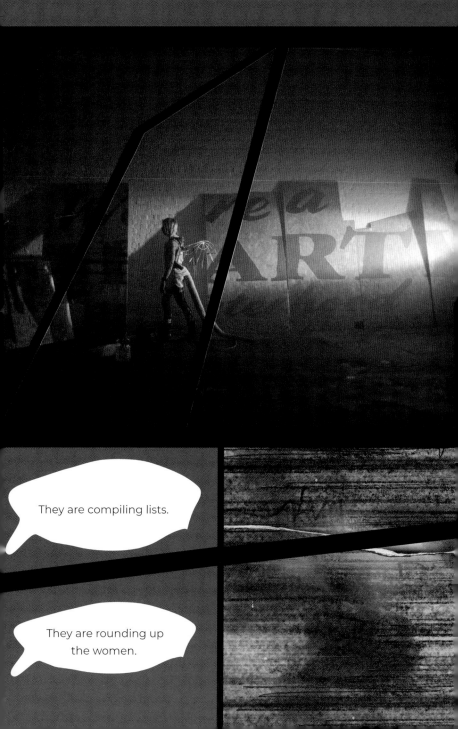

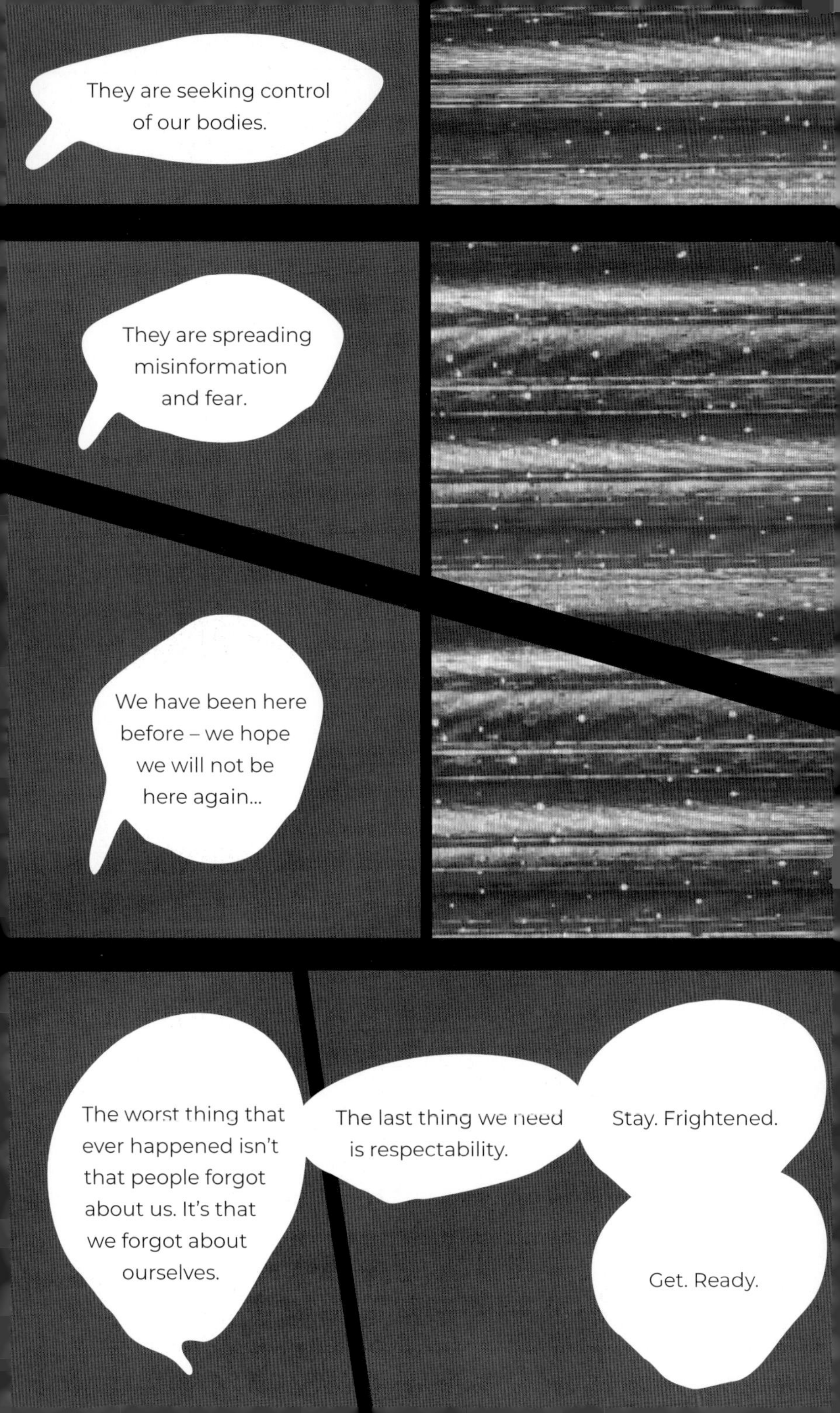
They are seeking control of our bodies.
They are spreading misinformation and fear.
We have been here before – we hope we will not be here again...
The worst thing that ever happened isn't that people forgot about us. It's that we forgot about ourselves.
The last thing we need is respectability.
Stay. Frightened.
Get. Ready.

WHAT DO I WANT?
WHAT DO I WANT?

A prosthetic that makes me run slower
that alters my shape
that makes my hair grow longer and faster and thicker

that makes my skin grow soft
that stops me ageing

that offers me protection
that gives me power
that means when you touch me I don't just feel it here, but here and here and here and here and here, a surging wave that envelopes my entire body.

Sometimes I feel like I could shoot fire from my fingertips...
So natural, like breathing.

*Emma sings karaoke a second time – it is 'Groove is in the Heart' again, but it plays at double speed.*

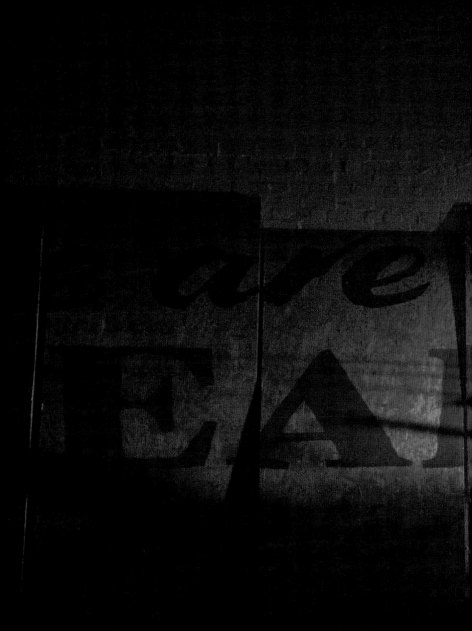

# CYCLE 3
## BEGINS

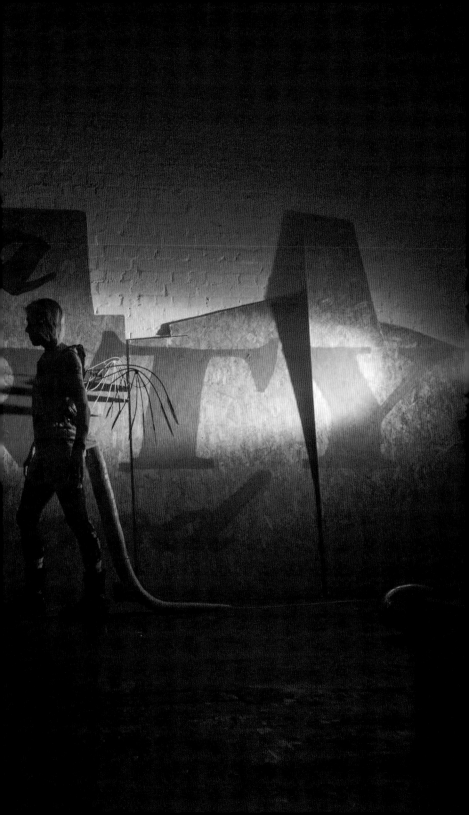

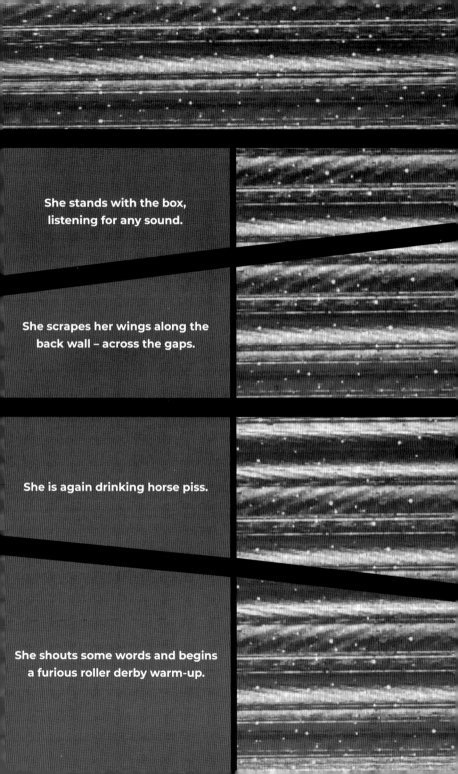

She stands with the box,
listening for any sound.

She scrapes her wings along the
back wall – across the gaps.

She is again drinking horse piss.

She shouts some words and begins
a furious roller derby warm-up.

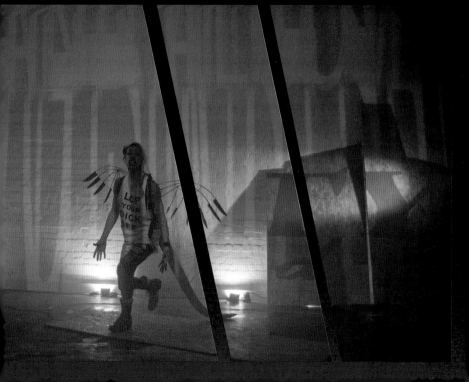

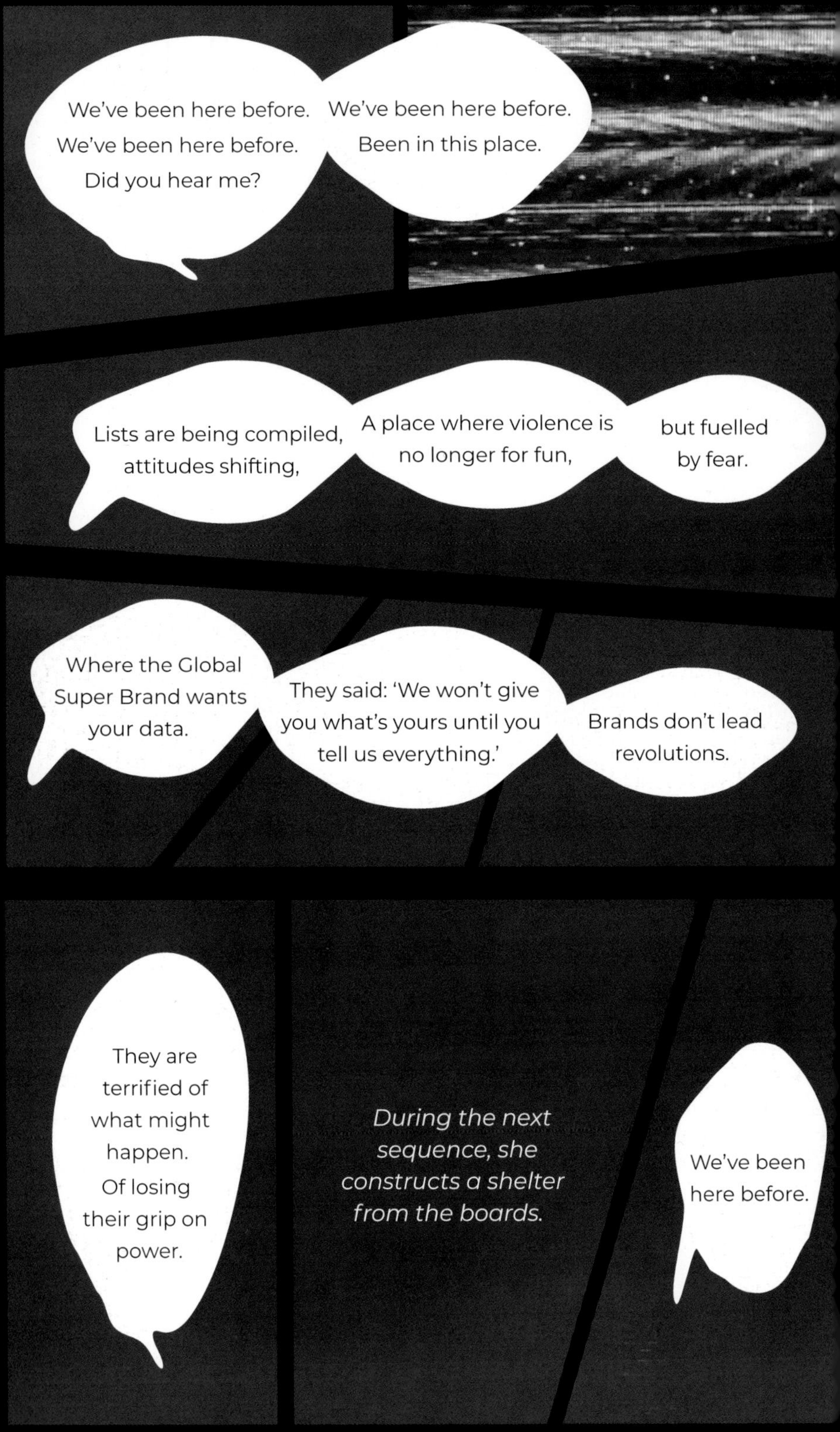
We've been here before. We've been here before. Did you hear me?
We've been here before. Been in this place.
Lists are being compiled, attitudes shifting,
A place where violence is no longer for fun,
but fuelled by fear.
Where the Global Super Brand wants your data.
They said: 'We won't give you what's yours until you tell us everything.'
Brands don't lead revolutions.
They are terrified of what might happen. Of losing their grip on power.
During the next sequence, she constructs a shelter from the boards.
We've been here before.

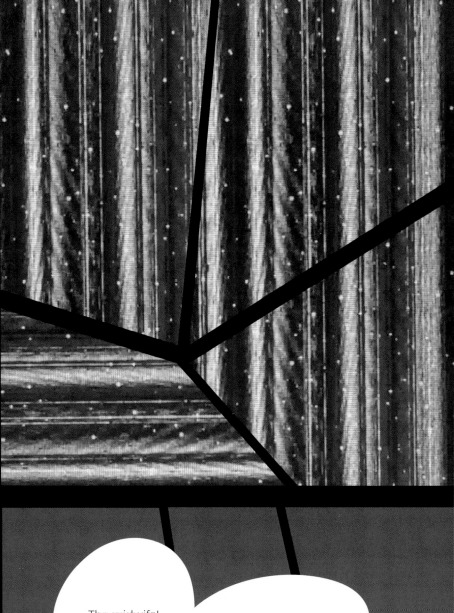

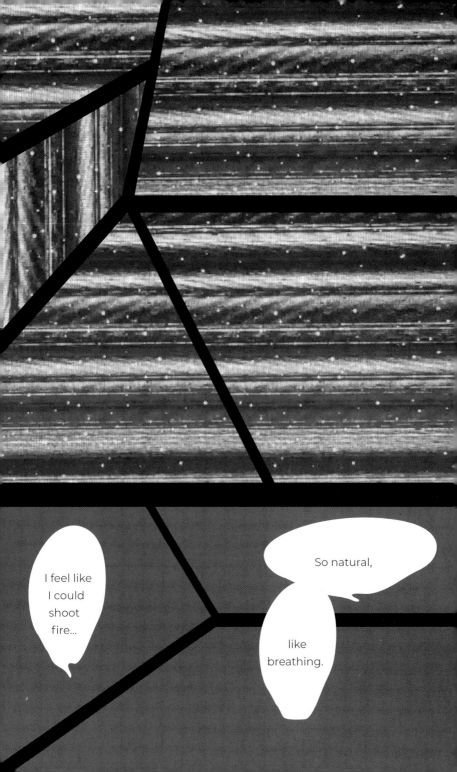

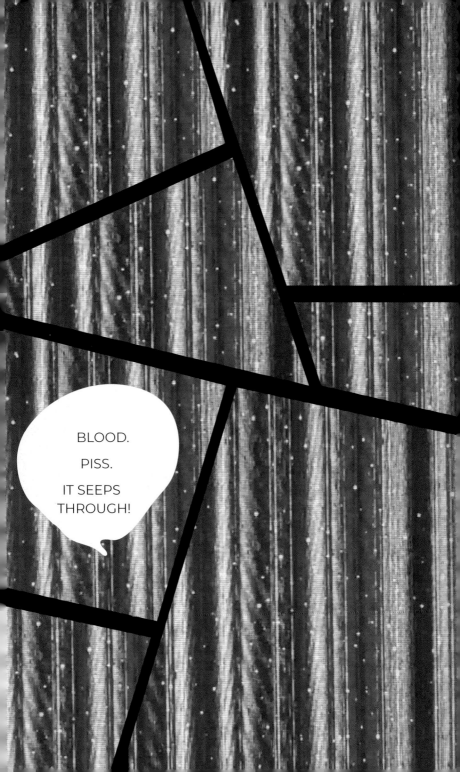

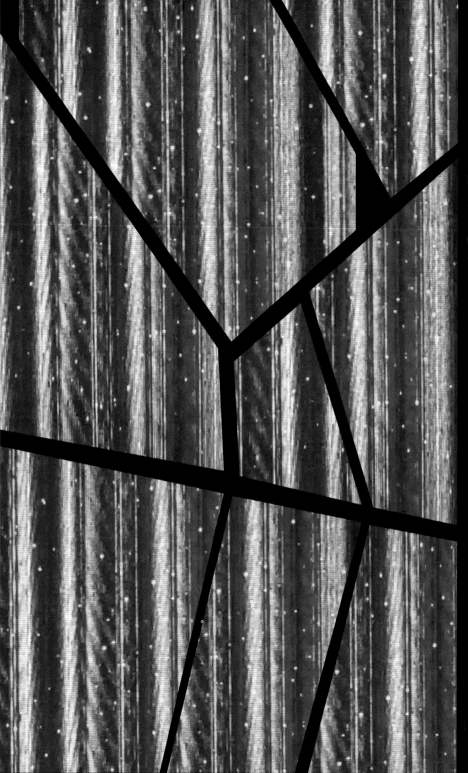

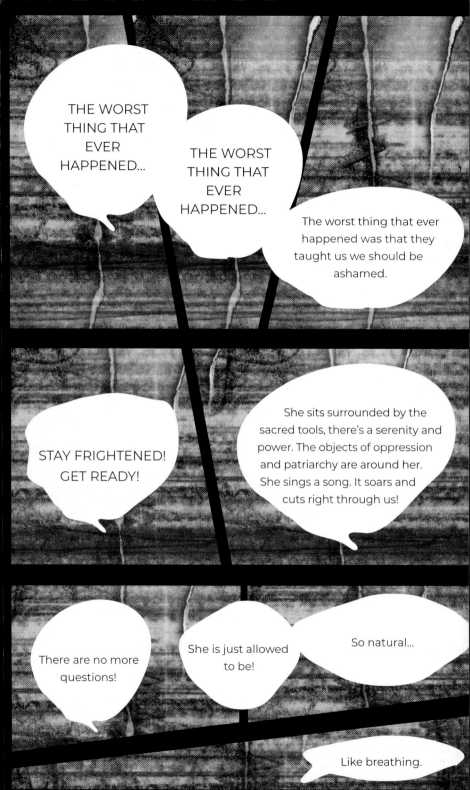

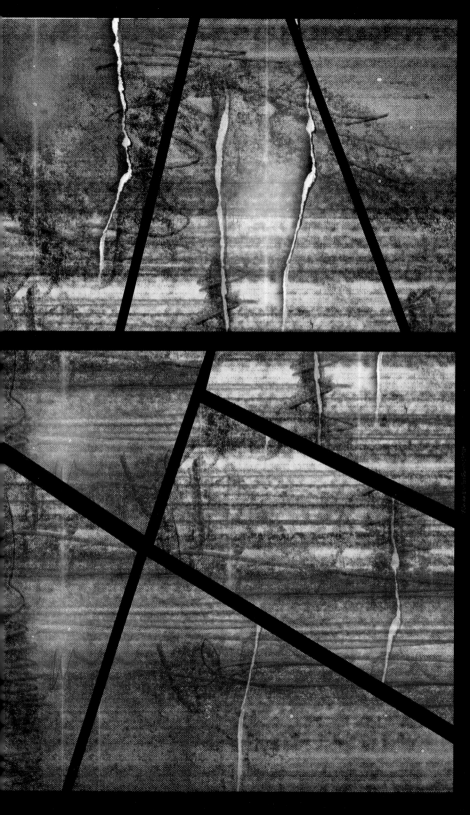

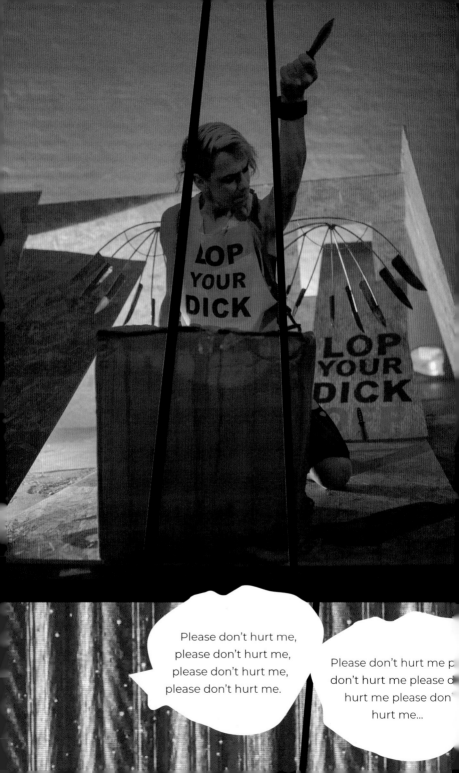

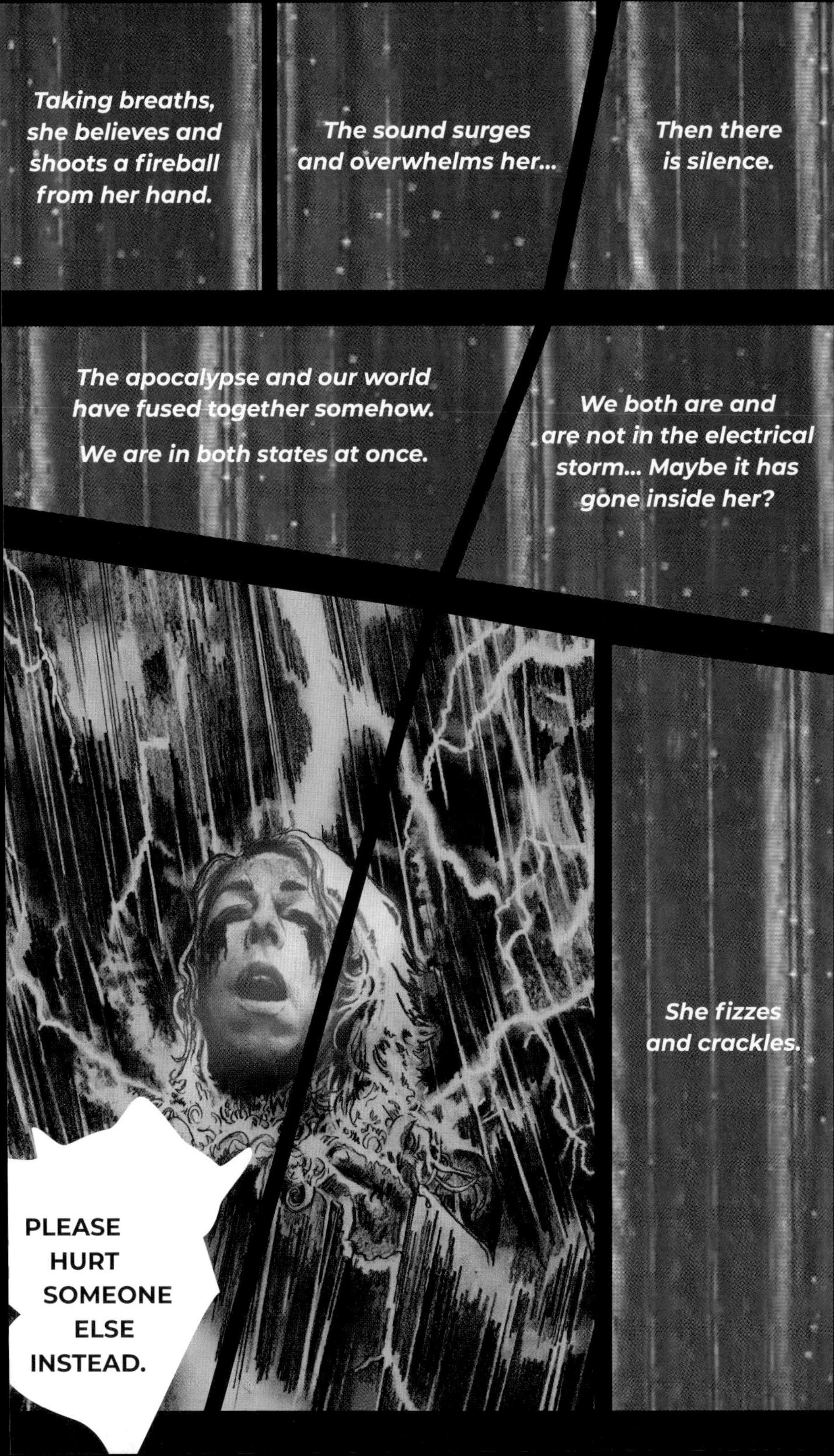
Taking breaths, she believes and shoots a fireball from her hand.
The sound surges and overwhelms her...
Then there is silence.
The apocalypse and our world have fused together somehow.
We are in both states at once.
We both are and are not in the electrical storm... Maybe it has gone inside her?
PLEASE HURT SOMEONE ELSE INSTEAD.
She fizzes and crackles.

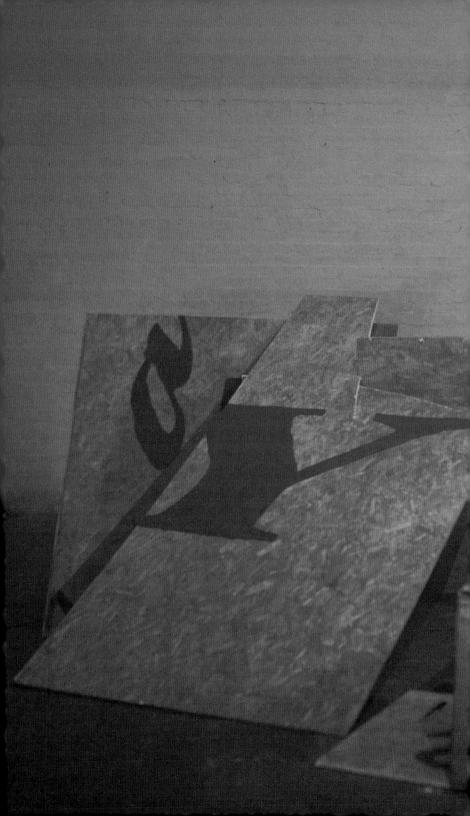

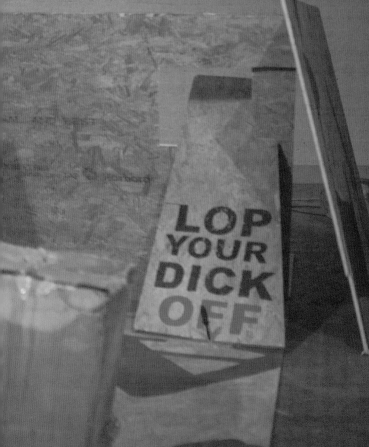

# CYCLE 4

She scrapes her wings
along the back wall.

Emma is outside
the structure.
She stands by the box.

She calmly drinks horse piss.

She begins a gentle
roller derby warm-up.

We've been here before.
We've been here before.
We've been here before.
We've been here before.

Been in this place.

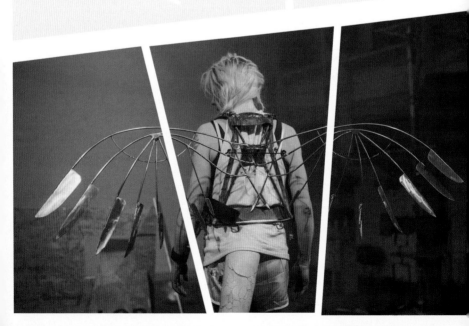

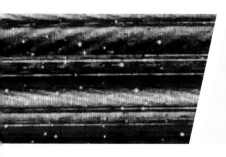

*She at last opens the box.*

*Slogan: 'I AM CAUGHT BETWEEN HEALING*
*AND VENGEANCE.'*

*She sings.*

If something disgusts you, I do it.
The worst shameful feeling, I now read as an invitation
To something that will be meaningful and beautiful and right.

THE SHAME OF IT,

I EMBRACE THE SHAME OF IT.

If someone disgusts you, I love them.
This other brave person, is my sister,
And we don't have to look to the past, no,
We don't have to look very far
To see that we have been here before
To see that they are living now.

THE SHAME OF IT,

I EMBRACE THE SHAME OF IT.

I will walk in fur and jewels,
Dripping with gold and stolen health
And with all of this beauty
I will stand on the highest chair and shout

WE

HAVE HEART.

ARE YOU FRIGHTENED NOW?

What do I ask of nature?
I embrace sensuality in a body that is changing.
There's nothing you can take from us
Nothing you can give to us
That we cannot find for ourselves.

THE SHAME OF IT,

I EMBRACE THE SHAME OF IT.

*She sets the box on fire. It becomes a magic fire – something where potions would be created – not destruction, but a fire of creation.*

*She settles herself behind it and her features change – the ancestors appear on the walls and the air tastes different.*

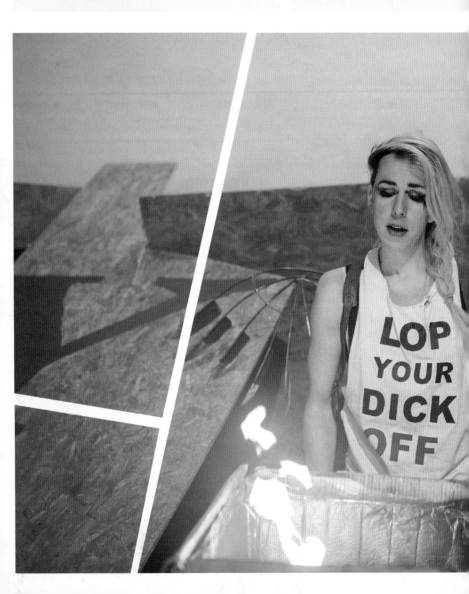

She fires shots into the air so the ceiling collapses and she will fight with the strength she has and she is complicated and strong and she relies on the strength of others and she will behave in a manner that makes her feel real...

She refuses to endure.

She has endured for long enough.

She refuses to endure.

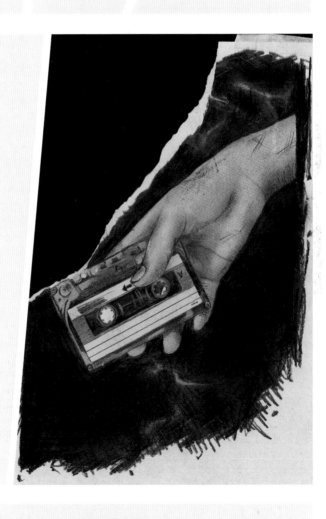

*Emma exits whistling – she returns, collects the tape cassette from the recorder and exits again. End.*

# AFTERWORD / WHAT'S NEXT?
In conversation with Travis Alabanza, March 2019

'I think we always see people put blame on certain groups when big amounts of change are happening, and who represents change and the power of change more than any other group? Trans people.'

This book has been an exercise in reflection – both personal and broadly political. I've been resistant to frame it as something new; however hard it may be to uncover archives of trans performance, they do exist. But I'm glad this volume of performance texts will continue that legacy – to better document the work of trans artists. To provide a place for our community to grow, to develop our art, personally and as a genre. To begin to ask: what does trans performance look like, when it is liberated from cis interpretation? When it strays beyond autobiography? I don't know what that looks like yet, but we'll be finding out soon.

So. What's next? And first, where are we now? What exactly has changed in the UK since this project began? Trans rights haven't changed all that much officially, which is a concern when public attitude and demand for services have dramatically altered. Gender non-conforming people are in theory protected by law as we were then (the last big change was the Equality Act in 2010), yet we still experience discrimination; Gender Identity Clinics are available to access through the NHS, but demand means waiting times are untenable. In 2018, five thousand people marched at Trans Pride Brighton without incident, yet the same year at London Pride a group of anti-trans campaigners were permitted to lead the march. There is more intense media scrutiny of trans people, more vocal and active opposition; but we also have a more nuanced articulation of the many experiences of being trans – within the trans community at least. We are moving beyond the reductive born-in-the-wrong-body trope to an understanding that we are not the problem – the world around us is. Non-binary people have become a much more vocal part of the trans community, with more people identifying as non-binary in the recent Gender Recognition Act survey than trans men or trans women.

**EMMA** I have been reflecting on my work. I have been looking back at the last seven years and how that has been in a... I don't like to use a phrase that makes it seem new, it's a remembering, right? In Western society – in the UK and in North America – there has been a cultural remembering of trans identity. But it's been quite a rollercoaster ride and we are currently in 2019 – what's happening now?

**TRAVIS** I think if we are just focusing on the West, on where we are geographically, I feel like these last two years... I mean, I came in when it felt like the rollercoaster was already happening – maybe that's why people know who I am, because the rollercoaster was already in motion. I feel like the last two years for me [have] been a combination of what happens when a group gets thrusted into more voice and has more eyes on them, and we are currently watching how a country responds to that and as we've seen it's not positive. What we are seeing is like, visibility markers of success without actual cultural shifts or economic shifts that are changing every day. I would call the last three years 'trans capitalism', basically. I think we are being fooled into thinking we are getting better because we have more magazine covers and campaigns, but actually waiting times have gone up, unemployment has gone up. Harassment has gone up. We are in this false limbo. In the last two years what has defined the trans experience in the UK has been the press. I don't know how it was before...

**EMMA** It wasn't like this before. Sometimes I think to myself, 'Am I just being dramatic? Is this in my head?'

UK laws haven't changed much in the last seven years, but they might – and it might not be in our favour. With uncertain results to the Gender Recognition Act consultation, trans charities subjected to funding reviews, even a threatened repeal of the Human Rights Act, there is an opposition that didn't use to be there, catalysed by grossly biased media overexposure. Huge platforms in newspapers and broadcast media are being given to faux debates and views that wouldn't have been acceptable a decade ago. And just because things didn't change much in the last seven years, doesn't mean they won't. It is lazy to assume that trans rights are on some inevitable upward progression. Contemporary events do not necessarily hold that up. It is certainly a possibility that the lives of trans people will vastly improve in the next seven years – I am hopeful – but it will only happen if we all work towards that goal now.

**EMMA** Certainly the last couple of years it has felt like the press could just print stuff that was not true and get away with it.

**TRAVIS** The standard of it... I hate when people say, 'Imagine if this was said about...' I think it is useful sometimes to say that this could not be said about certain people without fact-checking. And that's what we've lost in the press – they are just printing lies. I think it has really defined the last years. When I travel for work to the States – even where we know there are so many laws being put in place by their new president – they still say, 'At least I'm not in the UK because of the press.'

**EMMA** Which is incredible because I think seven years ago there was a sense of, 'Thank goodness we are not in the States, because look at how messed up a lot of their things are and we don't have the bathroom problems and we don't have problems with the religious right.' And gradually what we've done is brought those issues that were not a thing and they've been gradually, insidiously made into a thing. So now the UK public have begun to think things are important that we have never thought [were] important.

**TRAVIS** I don't think it is a coincidence that this happened at the same time as Brexit. I don't think it is a coincidence that this happened at the same time as a huge political uncertainty. I think we always see people put blame on certain groups when big amounts of change are happening, and who represents change and the power of change more than any other group? Trans people. Who represents bodily autonomy and deciding what's what and having ownership over myself? (And anti-capitalism in a far stretch if we really wanna go down that way in theory?) Trans people. So I think it's really – when I saw it coming I thought, 'Of course, this country doesn't know what the fuck's up, it doesn't know what choices it's making, let's pin this huge level of fear on people who are making personal choices for themselves daily.'

I live in Brighton and I am blessed that my local community feels strong and supportive – but I realise I am lucky. I want to see trans people living and loving life, regardless of whether they live in a largely liberal town. More Trans Prides are appearing around the world, and we need mainstream prides to step up and show support for trans people, so we feel secure in our solidarity from the broader LGBQ+ community. We must foster the wonderful growth of grassroots trans organisations like Open Barbers, Mermaids and Gendered Intelligence. Trans people supporting each other and framing things on our terms.

**TRAVIS** I guess in five years I would love for our understanding of transness, to follow less rules of cisgender culture. I would love to see our understanding of each other go a bit beyond this A-B style of being trans. 'I was this and now I think I'm this.' And I would love that to inform the complexities of being trans. I think what we are doing at the moment is responding to pressure to be understood so we are making ourselves more simple than we are. So I would like to see us allow for more space to be complex. And I think how that would play out is that we would be having more conversations about why some of us are doing things to our bodies and being honest about how sometimes that comes from an innate want and how sometimes that comes from an innate need for safety, and how both of these things are valuable – and just having a bit more of an honest conversation about where we are and where we're at. I would hope, I don't know if in five years it would change, but I would hope that the streets would be safer for us. That is the real thing that gets left out in so many conversations, where actually it should be at the forefront of so many: that so many trans people, but specifically people who experience transmisogyny – whether they've medically transitioned or not, they know that feeling of being in between their medical transitions, or not quite how they want to be yet – and I think that people who have not experienced that, going out in the world in a dress, or in make-up, and people knowing that you weren't assigned female at birth... That's a non-stop harassment that I think people do not understand.

**EMMA** I think even on the good days where you can recognise that you are owning your truth, and feeling great – even on those days there'll be a moment in the day – even if it's not coming from anyone else...

**TRAVIS** It's coming from you and your memory and your past and I think, I hope, [that] in the next five years we start becoming – I hope we have a hangover effect from all this visibility that equals actual public compassion.

So what's next? Almost a decade on from that first morning at Ovalhouse, I will be returning with a performance called *We Dig*. It will be part of their Demolition Party season, a group of shows programmed to very literally demolish the building before they move to a new venue. *We Dig* will feature seventeen transfeminine performers over three weeks – a core international cast and a guest performer each night. And we are going to talk, and dance, and share stories, and dig. Each performance, we are going to excavate a massive hole. A literal representation of a community burying itself for safety and protection, uncovering lost knowledge and leaving traces for the future.

But while clubs and fringe venues are celebrating trans women and our experiences, unsurprisingly our work still sits outside the commercial mainstream. I say 'unsurprisingly' because to be an out trans woman *is* to be outside the mainstream – a political act – and because of who controls these theatres or film studios and their programmes. When our identities are represented, it's by cisgender actors – usually cisgender men. In a strange echo of the supposed all-male stages of Elizabethan theatre, we live in a time where it is more likely to see a cisgender man performing female impersonation than it is to see a trans woman playing herself.

In those same mainstream outlets, what trans representation we do see is also filtered through a cisgender lens: commissioned by, written by, directed by cisgender people. It's important that trans women's lives are widely portrayed, yes – but our myriad of stories should be told with authenticity and not through cis translation. I do not believe there are any circumstances where it is appropriate for a cisgender actor to be portraying a trans character; nor is it appropriate for cis actors to keep gaining awards and social capita for doing so.

> **TRAVIS** My dream is not to be cast in a cis role. My dream is for my transness not to disrupt a role in a way that means they won't give it to me. I want to be trans and be that role. I want to play a love interest but I don't want that love interest to be cis. I want to be trans playing that role.

Transgender actors exist. And when we are hard to find, it is the industry's responsibility to create training and opportunities for us to be easier to find in the future. Brazilian travesti actress and campaigner Renata Carvalho talks about art as a space of power and historical exclusion: how are trans people supposed to see ourselves in art if we do not see ourselves in the day-to-day running of theatre spaces either? Or in day-to-day life at all?

> **TRAVIS** I also hope that in five years, trans people... I'm proud of transness, I love talking about transness, I don't want to pass, my goal isn't to hide – but I hope that people who have that as a goal and want to be able to just exist and trans be part of their identity, like having brown hair is, can do that.

> **EMMA** I just hope that doesn't feel like hiding. Someone said to me recently at an industry thing – a casting director said about a client who had finally been cast as a cis person said to me, 'Well that's the dream isn't it?' And it's *a* dream – it's that person's

dream. But my dream is not to play a cis woman. It's not my dream to be a cis woman. Well if I could push a button and have that easy ride I wouldn't wish to be a cis man... But my dream isn't to play a cis woman and 'trick' people. That idea outside the trans community is so predominant that everyone assumes that is what we want.

**TRAVIS** People don't understand the expansions we could have. There's so much experience of trans people doing the work of cis gatekeeping to us and I hope that stops too. One thing that being trans teaches you so quickly is that assumptions and assuming... We are still guilty of, when we see someone, assuming that's the version of them that they wanted to be today, right? There's so many factors that go into that...

**EMMA** I think what we're saying is a step back towards complexity. We have really lost our taste for complex.

In the UK, censorship of authentic trans narratives seems systematic but inadvertent, yet in other parts of the world trans people keep experiencing physical danger and a dramatic loss of privileges. We are seeing state censorship interfering with trans-led performance. The title alone of British writer Jo Clifford's play *The Gospel According to Jesus, Queen of Heaven* has been enough to see it banned in several countries, and in 2018 an entire festival in Rio de Janeiro was cancelled when the state censor refused to allow the play to go on. The performance, which imagines Jesus as a trans woman (played in Brazil by Renata Carvalho), was relocated to a public space. Queues formed around the block to see the show, which was then performed twice because of the demand. On another occasion, the venue was literally dismantled during the show in an attempt to disrupt the performance, as producer Natalia Mallo described in a Facebook post:

*'You have hours when you live or you shoot. At halftime, a bang and a lot of smoke. Then, after releasing bombs in the space, there arrived a judicial injunction asking for another cancellation, and we decided to disobey. The contracted security turned against us, and forbid the public's entry. Well friend, Renata Carvalho said:*

'Enough!' She broke everything (it's not a metaphor), exposed the cowards and screamed all truths. The force was so much that an entire battalion did not have the courage to act. 'Calm her down!' they yelled at me, and I thought: 'No. Listen, and hold!' It was quite cathartic. Renata opened the gates by force and asked for the invasion of the public, who occupied the space to the screams of, 'Fascists!' We tore up the injunction, and we began the show. They cut the sound, so we sang the soundtrack. They cut the lights. They took the awning that protected the audience from the rain, and the play didn't stop. The public stayed until the end, and was our protection. Now, when we think it's over, a new decision calls again for inclusion in the festival's schedule asking for it to be presented tomorrow. Scenes for the next chapter. What a phase.'

The 'Trans Tipping Point' didn't just occur in 2014 – we are still teetering. It is impossible to say which way we'll tip. But we should be prepared to fight for it like our Brazilian friends.

> **EMMA** And that risk shouldn't be... We should take creative risks, always, otherwise what's the fucking point? But I think in the immediate next five years there is a risk that has to be taken by venues and funding bodies. Because there aren't enough of us – aren't *any* of us that have that power at all.

> **TRAVIS** And we'd know them.

> **EMMA** And hopefully in ten years there's a whole bunch of us and we all keep marching on and we will be in positions to do these things and that's where I want to put my energy. I want to keep making work and I want to keep making work with trans people and see what happens.

Trans performance, and the ways in which trans artists are making performance, is constantly evolving too. Thanks to an episode of the brilliant podcast *Woodland Secrets* several years ago, my attention was drawn by novelist Imogen Binnie to a concept first articulated in Elaine Showalter's book *A Literature of Their Own*, which suggests that minorities or subcultures within our society make art about themselves in three separate stages. From trying to find common ground with the majority culture ('Look at all the ways in which we are the same. Please don't hurt us') through an outright rejection of it ('We are *nothing* like you'), on to the third and final stage – 'You don't matter.' The culmination is all about inward-looking self-discovery, rather than in relation to the mainstream – whether in opposition or allegiance.

**TRAVIS** I want to see way more complex – I want to see work that is not just having a trans story, but is made through and through with trans people. I also want to see trans people doing stuff that obviously their transness has informed, but isn't a story or narrative for cis people to understand trans issues. I want to push beyond work whose goal is to make us understood and push into work that is what this artist wants to make, and how is their transness informing that and reflecting that. I think we saw this with Black theatre. I want to see work that [allows us] to be grotesque, nasty, comical, challenging and flawed. Because there is still a pressure, a nervousness attached to us being anything other than nice. I want to just see more risk and more fun, I want to see more inward collaboration that like, isn't about the theatre looking great, isn't about that commercial success...

**EMMA** I was smiling because it's such a simple wish and I feel like this has been articulated so many times in so many contexts and I can't believe that that's still the dream. And it's still not happening and even the really progressive projects that I get invited to be a part of are still led by cis people or directed by cis people, or gate-kept by cis people who probably don't think that's what they are doing. Because they probably are the 'good ones'. But yeah, I don't even know what it looks like to have a whole theatre full of trans people working on a show in every aspect of it because we never got to do it...

**TRAVIS** I don't know many trans actors, I don't know many trans set designers –

**EMMA** And part of that is finding people and upskilling and giving others opportunities and finding what that language and what that voice is, and away from autobiography!

**TRAVIS** Away from autobiography PLEASE!

**EMMA** Says someone who has spent the last seven years making autobiographical work!

Much of my recent inspiration has come from the learning I have been privileged to receive from trans women in countries outside of the UK, yet most of the performances in this volume stem from my experience as a white, British trans woman, in a culture that has drawn heavily from North American contemporary understanding of gender diversity. I want us to share knowledge further and learn from trans groups around the world. I think we could liberate each other.

I have been reminded of how totally amazing trans people are – how much strength, resilience and determination have brought us to where we are today. I don't resort to hyperbole here – trans people are Strong, Resilient and Determined. Although our day-to-day lives differ greatly, there is a shared bond that is extremely powerful. Every time I meet a trans person there is an exciting moment where we celebrate each other for just existing. Against the odds. Each of us, no matter our social status today, began this journey alone, questioning ourselves – battling shame and self-doubt and stepping against the flow of family, friends, religion and governments – to insist that we know ourselves best and that we are not wrong.

And so every time I meet another trans person is a moment of pure joy, because they are one more person who understands; one more point of proof that what I knew to be true when I was a child was, in fact, true. In Indonesia, I was taught the secret greeting that calabai use to greet each other. I love that a single word and a gesture can contain so much that is unspoken.

It seems fitting to conclude this book the same way the project began: by being a parent. It is the most directly political act of my life, and I feel so proud when I see Joey educating others and being visible. He once said to a stranger on a bus:

*'My Daddy plays roller derby.'*
*'Does he?'*

*'My Daddy is a lady and some Daddies are ladies and did you know that some men can marry men and some women can marry women... And some people are a 'they'. Well, now they know everything.'*

He never mis-pronouns me. 'Daddy' is a female term to us. He is naturally drawn to be fluid in clothes and style of play. And really it seems an obvious choice that, when confronted with two sides of a shop – one full of bright-coloured clothes with rainbows and one full of identical beige, grey and navy clothes – one would choose the sparkles, despite the temptation of the occasional T-Rex.

What happens when a kid grows up with all this as their norm? It's been so interesting to watch Joey understand my gender identity and that of his many trans and genderqueer uncles and aunties. He fully understands that the decisions we make are transgressive, but the only behaviour he frames as 'unnatural' is that of certain relatives who have tried (unsuccessfully) to impress on him binary ideas of 'boy' and 'girl'. Despite its ubiquity, the gender binary is a hard concept to understand, and it was impossible to spot where he picked it up. But he was happy to unlearn.

> **EMMA** So I've got a little boy. Well I have a little person who's actually interestingly articulating their gender in two ways at the moment. One is 'boy' and Joey says that for now he's a boy and he likes to be called 'he' and that's fine. But also that really his gender is nothing and he's not a 'he' or 'she' or 'they', he's just Joey. And sometimes he asks for his name to be his pronoun, which is so sophisticated and blows my mind that that's where he is at six! And that's what comes of having known a lot of gender non-conforming people in his life in a meaningful way. And I think actually it's quite cool for a child to go, 'My gender identity is "child".' That feels really appropriate.

I want to say thank you to everyone who has helped me put these thoughts and times together in one place – it's been a ride to reflect on the events of the last few years, and I'm ecstatic to be able to bring it all into one place. I talk about using this book as a historical document, a time capsule for *a* trans experience, but let's also use it as a current one. These plays scratch the surface of what is happening. Let's go deeper together, and move forward together.

> **EMMA** I always like to think about what the role of an artist is. I think it's a really sacred position, and actually politics isn't one of our remits. We can inform and we can advise – and being in Indonesia recently, sitting with the Bissu shamans there – their history goes back forever, and they were really into the monarchy, and I was told by everyone that our position is to sit at the side of the king and be their advisor. And I think that as an artist, I don't want to be a policy-maker. I am not a politician. Politician should be another sacred job where you are really good at representing people and hearing them and being a focus that can make positive change. 'Politician' shouldn't be a dirty word, it should be a useful civic person. And I'm an artist – I want to serve the greater good in a different way.

> **TRAVIS** My work has political power and I'm a political person so my work will always be that, but I want the craft to be what's there, and the change what comes from that... Now I am interested in – what's the funding that being an artist can access that [I] can then spread out? How can I use the access I do have and the comfortable places I do have to spread this out?

A final thank you to my trans (including non-binary) siblings and queer allies around the world. I may not know you personally, but your existence has held and informed me, gently corrected me, helped me along my journey and kept me going on countless occasions. Your blogs, poems, Facebook rants, Instagram posts, Tumblr memes, Flickr selfies, righteous songs, YouTube timeline videos, books of memoir and books of trans-apocalyptic science fiction, lectures and speeches (at Pride rallies and in chat rooms) have helped me feel real.

Thank you.

Let's keep going.

# THANKS AND ACKNOWLEDGEMENTS

*None of Us is Yet a Robot* was made in collaboration with Abby Butcher. Significant collaborators across all five projects were Keir Cooper, Ivor MacAskill, Rachel Mars and Myriddin Pharo.

A huge debt of gratitude is due to Oberon Books for publishing these texts and in particular Serena Grasso and Konstantinos Vasdekis, whose talent, encouragement and enthusiasm for this book has made it a joy to put together.

All productions were supported using public funding by the National Lottery through Arts Council England.

### Language
Dramaturgy – Rachel Mars
Original music – Keir Cooper
Lighting Design – Anna Barrett

With tremendous thanks to Nick, Rosana and the entire team at Buzzcut where this piece was first presented. To Ovalhouse Theatre and Shoreditch Town Hall for the space and time, Dave Dodd for the *Blue Peter* dubstep and Morganic for graffiti lessons. Thank you to Myriddin Pharo, Tin Shed Scenery, Rosie Powell Photography and Will Brady. To Gendered Intelligence and Open Barbers. Very special thanks to Felix Lane for inspiration and support.

### Doodle
Thanks to Isolde Godfrey for art consultation, to all at Buzzcut Festival and Forest Fringe. Maddy Costa and Dialogue Festival. Mary Patterson, Ross Osborne and Something Other.

### egg/box
Thanks to Patricia Rodriguez, Nigel Barrett and Gwendolyn Scott for their voices. To Rachel Mars, Rosana Cade, Chiron Stamp and Carlos Otero for dramaturgy; to Buzzcut Festival, Forest Fringe, The Campsite, Jerwood Charitable Foundation, Cove Park and Fuel for development time and space.

## Rituals for Change

Made in collaboration with Abby Butcher, Ivor MacAskill and Myriddin Pharo, with help from Rachel Blackman and original music from Keir Cooper.

Overwhelming thanks to: Pink Fringe and the Marlborough Theatre, Kirsty Cotton and Hall for Cornwall Creation Space, The Spire Arts, South Street Arts Centre, Ovalhouse, Forest Fringe, Wildworks, Chris Goode and Company and all at Open House Riot Act, Rachel Mars, Dan Cheyne, Will Brady, Yvonne K Strain, Sheran Dickinson and Liz Ridgway.

A full version of *Rituals for Change* can be found online at **bit.ly/ritualsforchange** with award-winning cinematography from Rosie Powell and art direction by Myriddin Pharo. Huge thanks to Abby Butcher, Keir Cooper, Mel Sanson and Subira Wahogo.

The film was made possible with funding through The Space and Arts Council England.

## Hearty

Design – Myriddin Pharo
Lighting and Projections – Joshua Pharo
Music – Anthea Clark
Original Songs – Vicky Abbott

With thanks to Pri Bertucci and SSEX BBOX Festival, British Council Indonesia and Tamara Pertamina, Hall for Cornwall Creation Space and the Yard Theatre, Rachael Clerke and Ivor MacAskill, Piers Mason, Lucia Gomez and the Spire, Brighton. Thanks to Travis Alabanza, Jacqueline Gomes de Jesus, Tamara Pertamina, Selina Thompson and Angela Clerkin.

I wanted to give us some space
because there can be alot going on out there
and there."s some things I wanted to say to YOU.

First up (and this might be hard to hear) but
you are beautiful.

yeah,yeah, I know... but you are. Beautiful.

- try not to hold yourself to cis beauty ideals,
(but understand it"s ok to do this too)

- BE KIND TO YOURSELF

- I don't know your history, but chances are you
feel more vulnerable now than the world brought you
up to feel. That"s OK. Don't be scared but be sensible.
Look after yourself and allow others to look after u too.

- Trust other trans women, seek out other trans women,

(it took me ages to learn this because I was frightend,
of not being trans enough, woman enough, femme enough,
pretty enough, radical enough...)

YOU. ARE. ENOUGH.

It is OK to take up space.
It is OK to be tough, to be strong.
It is OK to be vulnerable and it is definitely OK
to ask for help.

WE are a HEARTY sisterhood.

I love you. xx

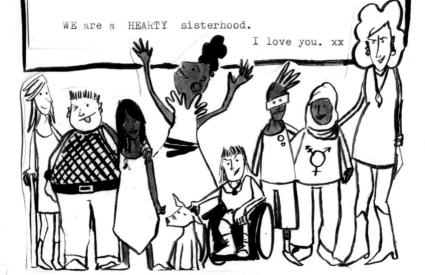